June 20, 2018

We
As A **Black** People

"Our Time Has Come!"

TO: M. Granberry
From: Clinton L. Black

I appreciate your support and I hope you enjoy my new book.

4-3-99

Black, Clinton L.
We As A Black People

Copyright ©1998. All rights reserved. No part of this book may be reproduced or utilized in any form or by any means, electronic or mechanical, including photocopying, recording or by any information storage and retrieval system, without permission in writing from the author. Inquiries should be addressed to:

Clinton Black
Post Office Box 9096
Fort Lauderdale, Florida 33310

10987654321
Copyright ©1998 by Clinton L. Black
ISBN: 0-9620180-1-5
Library of Congress Catalog Card Number: 90-93252
Published 1999 in the United States of America by Clinton L. Black

New York • Washington, D.C. • Chicago • Los Angeles
Cape Town • Tokyo • Paris

In Dedication

This book is proudly dedicated to every Native American and African slave who ever lived in the United States.

Table of Contents

Thank You i
Acknowledgements ii
About *"We As A Black People"* iii
About Clinton iv

PART I • ESSAYS

The Black Experience
Jesus Christ Was Black... 1
Financial Fairness.. 3
Crime and Consequences 5
Whence We Came.. 6

Civil Rights
The Most Segregated City In The South..................... 8
Where Is "America"?.. 11
Where To Go From Here... 13

Narrative
My Special Observance of Dr. Leffall's Return To FAMU 15

Miscellaneous
The Viewing of Halley's Comet 20
Chrono.. 22
Let's Face It...23

Philosophy and Religion
Merry Christmas?... 25
Life After Death Exists.. 28

Black History
African Americans of Distinction 30

A Letter
Dear Dr. King... 38

Biography
Mr. Claude Neal 43
T. Thomas Fortune... 46

PART II • POEMS, LYRICS, RAPS, QUOTES AND A PLAY
— Holidays and Celebrations —

Rev., Dr. Martin Luther King, Jr. January 15
I Dreamt I Saw The King 53

Thanksgiving Last Thursday in November
This Day Of Thanks 53
This Is Thanksgiving 54

Christmas December 25
How The Word, Christmas, Came To Be 55

Christmas Is Coming!.. 56
Christmas Is Here!! 57
My Christmas With Bill Cosby................................. 59
My Christmas Day 61

A Christmas Play
Billy Boy, Please Come Home For Christmas.............. 64

Love
I Love You 68
You Are So Charming.. 68
Just For Your Love 70
I Want You To Notice Me 71
I Just Want To Get To Know You............................ 72
Give A Man A Chance.. 73
Lady, Let's Touch 74
You're The Only One In My World........................... 76
All I Need Is You... 77
A Love Like Yours... 78
A Certain One 79
A Man Who's Still In Love With You........................ 80
Since The First Time I Saw You 81
Since You Left Me, Lady 82
Everything Is All Right... 83
I Love You For What You Are.................................. 84
No One... 84
You Are My Lady 85
To Have A Devoted Man 86
Don't Know Much...87

Marriage
The Only Time, I 88
The Only Time, II 89
Our Love Has To Change.. 91
Since We've Been Married....................................... 92
Let's Save Our Marriage 93
What Am I Without You?... 95

Personal
"Hello" 96
Mommy's Little Love... 97
I Want To Thank You... 98
A Friend Like You.. 99
What Matters To Me.. 100
I Want To Go Back Home 100
My Struggle Is Too Great.. 101

If You Believe In Yourself 101
Just The Feel Of A Hand 102
A Lonely Saturday Night 103
This Life, Alone 105
My Troubles Are Endless 106
When Grandma Is Gonnnnn 106

Rap
Kids Just Don't Understand 107
Play My Hit Again! 109

Social
Out On The Job 112
Hard Working People (Like Us) 113
My Little Smoking Song 114
Because Times Are Real Bad 116
The Other Side Of The Computer 117
Our Children 119
Children Learn What They Live 120
... When You're Dead In Your Grave! 121

African American
...For Black People To Do? 122

Religion
To Fall In Love, With Living 124
My Love Was Gone 125
How Did God Do It? 126
I'm Singing A Nervous Song, Jesus 127
Until I Can Pray No More 128
II ? or Not II ? 129

Philosophy
Life 130
Everybody Has A Story To Tell 131
The Whereabouts Of The Once-Lived 132
We're All The Same 133
Where Do We Go From Here? 134
_____(untitled)_____ 135
Time Is Passing By 137
... And Death 137

Quotes
Quotes by Clinton 140

We As A Black People Order Form 141

Thank You!

I would like to express my profound thanks and appreciation to you for your wise selection in reading my new book.

May I offer you a challenge to write and publish in your respective area(s) of interest or specialty? Really, it's just that simple to apply your thoughts to a writing pad. If I can do it, surely, YOU CAN!

Please do take your time to enjoy this most enchanting collection of lyrics, poems and essays, and feel perfectly free to share it with your family, friends, guests and all others. May God bless you... never give up.

Acknowledgements

Foremostly, I acknowledge Jesus Christ for making everything possible.

As earnestly as I would like to, I cannot list all of the many individual people who have proven supportive and influential to me in my growth and development as a person and as a writer. I do, nonetheless, ask that each respective individual recognize their acknowledgement and accept it with all the honor in which it is offered.

About "We As A Black People"

This new book is a felicitous collection of encouraging true stories, essays, poems and lyrics. Also included in this new book is a most inspiring Christmas play, which I recently composed.

My first two books consist primarily of poems and lyrics. However, I have included unforgettable stories and essays in this new book with the intention of giving my readers an enhanced understanding of my unique style of writing. Although I write on a variety of subjects, I am strikingly disciplined in maintaining my signature mode of expression in everything I write.

This remarkable new book is different. It's practical contents vary from how to obtain a loan from your credit union or bank to proving that Jesus Christ was Black. I write on various subjects because I believe that every entity in the universe has an ultimate relation and connection. This will be more easily explained in the informative and moving literature you are about to read. I love to write and trust that you will love reading what I have written for you.

My next book is about explaining and proving the origin and only purpose of human life. Not yet titled, this forthcoming book will be a religion and high tech science-based educator and is scheduled to be published in 2000.

About Clinton

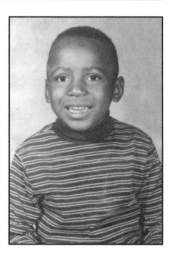

Clinton Leander Black was born on a cool Tuesday night, May 30, 1967, in the sleepy hamlet of Grand Ridge (Jackson County), Florida. He is the seventh child of Mr. Oscar Lee Black, Sr. and Mrs. Cojean Delores Gilbert Black's ten children. Grand Ridge is located fifty miles west of Florida's capital city, Tallahassee. Clinton was actually born in a tiny concrete home, which still stands today in rural Grand Ridge, and was delivered by a midwife.

As an infant growing up in Marianna (seven miles west of Grand Ridge) in the Poplar Springs Community, Clinton suffered from chronic asthma. Nevertheless, he was an unusually active, yet careful, child. One evening, when Clinton was four years old, he was playing in his family's yard. He ran too hard and suffered a near fatal asthma attack. However, he slowly grew out of his asthmatic condition.

Before the age of five, Clinton remembers little about his life but freshly recalls the eventful years thereafter. In school, he was a below average student and showed no particular interest in his studies or other advancing activities. His handwriting was illegible until he was 13 years old.

An easily impressionable child with a crucially supple self-esteem, the routine realities of Clinton's every day life literally conditioned him to genuinely believe that he was inferior to White people. Devastatingly (but reversibly) damaging, Clinton could not fully free himself from these mental shackles until the day he enrolled into Florida A & M University.

In 1972, when Clinton was in kindergarten at Riverside Elementary School, his oldest sister gave him a quarter on the bus one morning to buy his snack at recess. When he arrived at school, he placed the quarter in his locker... until recess.

However, before recess, a White student named Tonya began to dramatize that she was missing a quarter. The teacher noticed a quarter in Clinton's locker and immediately gave it to Tonya. No amount of protesting by Clinton could convince the teacher to rightfully return the quarter to him. Tonya was happy. The teacher was happy. But Clinton was sad.

As unfair as the occasion really was, it taught Clinton a very realistic lesson that was a cold prelude to his life ahead. Not one who harbors hate or envy, Clinton has long forgiven Tonya and the teacher.

Raised on a meager farm, with a large family in a small home, low-income and scarce opportunities were lingering realities bluntly introduced to him up front in life. As a consequence, Clinton was usually restricted to his home, church and school. Running water and rest rooms were luxuries he did not enjoy at home until he was in high school. He departed his parents' "nest" when he was seventeen. At home, as a youth, Clinton spent long hours meticulously repairing and constructing old bicycles and mechanical and electrical items. Clinton understood electronics and actually exhausted many days taking electronic devices apart and reconstructing them.

Clinton developed an appreciation for the value of hard work and self-reliance early in life. He tried to buy the things he wanted and have some money in his own pocket, so he diligently tried to find a job. However, no one would hire him... he was only eleven years old. Not one to give up, Clinton took matters into his own hands. To earn his own money, Clinton sold fruit and vegetable seeds to people in his community. He also sold aluminum cans at the local junk yard and soft drink bottles at the supermarket in town. He even once operated a candy and ice cream store from his home. The job Clinton really wanted; however, was a paper route.

He tried to become a paper boy but there were no paper routes in his rural community. Realizing that his best chance of establishing a paper route would be down town Marianna, Clinton planned. Town was nine miles away from home and the middle school he attended was twelve miles away. So he ordered supplies of a newspaper called *Grit* and arranged to leave one of the bicycles he constructed, worn but capable, at a relative's house in town. After school, he walked those three miles to his bicycle and began his successful newspaper route from there.

Clinton loves people and received great pleasure from walking long distances down dusty roads to visit people in his community, especially the elderly. Ironically, some families in his community barred him from visiting their homes. As he grew older, more than a few people assured Clinton that he would *"never 'mount to anything in life."* Clinton lived next door to his church, Poplar Springs Baptist, and became baptized into the church at the age of thirteen.

Later on, when Clinton was fifteen, he was a participating athlete on the high school's football team. Although he loved playing football, he was forced to quit due to a severe burn sustained to his right leg in August 1983. The burn resulted from a gasoline explosion. While a senior in high school, he was rejected at every request for a prom date.

After a prolonged period of physical therapy and medical treatment, Clinton eventually regained full use of his badly burned leg. Notwithstanding, he decided to commit the remainder of his school term to working, science fair competitions, and improving his grades for his desired college education in the biological and medical sciences. He proudly flipped burgers at Wendy's for two years (1982-1984) to pay for his needed science equipment.

Clinton tried his hand at invention, too. The only invention he could muster any real practical use from was a bicycle heater he built for riding his bicycle in the winter months. At first, people laughed at him for constructing such a ridiculous contraption to a bicycle. But when they saw that it actually worked, his discouragers were stunned.

Accustomed to being laughed at whenever he introduces a new idea or take ambitious actions, Clinton almost always prevails. As strange as it may seem, he often expects discouragement and ridicule when he starts an unprecedented mission... statistically, it ends in accomplishment.

Although Clinton initially revealed a definite skill in mechanics and electronics, he performed professionally in his biological and environmental research and experiments during his junior and senior years in high school. For this, he was highly applauded. Clinton's high school environmental research and experiments were so well performed and honored, in fact, his county school board sponsored him to two consecutive International Science and Engineering Fairs. There, he competed against other high school students' science projects from all around the nation and the world. This distinguished achievement made Clinton the first African American student from Jackson County to excel to participation in an International Science and Engineering Fair. During Clinton's senior year in high school, he was listed in *Who's Who Among American High School Students*. He also earned academic scholarships from the American Cancer Society and the Florida A & M University (FAMU) Department of Physics. In fact, he had to cancel his plans to enter the Navy in order to accept his earned college scholarships.

Before Clinton began his freshman term at FAMU, he assisted in an Environmental Protection Agency well casings contamination research project in the analytical chemistry department at Florida State University. This program was conducted during the summer of 1985 in Tallahassee. Clinton also spent part of his summer participating in a 4-H counselor camp at Cherry Lake, in north central Florida.

While in college, Clinton definitely experienced some of his most rewarding adventures. While only a freshman, he began to write prodigiously and published a complete poetry anthology, *The Best of Clinton Black's Poems and Lyrics*, when he was eighteen years old. Clinton sold many copies of this book on FAMU's campus. During this same year, he recorded one of his original spiritual songs, *"A New Day Is Coming Soon"*, on a gospel album. Clinton sold many of the albums himself. Clinton was also a member of numerous clubs and organizations at his university, including the Seven Hills Toastmasters International organization and FAMU men and women track teams. He served as manager and traveled with the track team for three years. The traveling availed to him many inspiring opportunities that further strengthened his, now, insatiable thirst for knowledge. The National Association of Colored Women Clubs, Inc. awarded Clinton an additional scholarship during his sophomore term at FAMU.

In 1987, Clinton launched an ambitious personal mission to correct an egregious travesty of justice after a savage stabbing claimed the innocent life of a young African American student at the high school from which he (Clinton) graduated.

Clinton took out time from school to work at McDonald's and various other jobs to augment the financing of his desired college education. In 1988, he went to Jacksonville, Florida to work as a security officer to help pay for his studies at FAMU.

Less than a year elapsed before Clinton had written another poetry anthology. This exquisite collection of mind-stimulating, rhyming reading was, indeed, a powerful thrust in his professional and literary growth. This second book, *Lyrical And Poetic Literature From The Emotions of The Mind*, is available and/or on display at certain locations in the United States, today.

Clinton graduated from FAMU with a Bachelors of Science Degree in biology/premedicine in 1993. He studied science and education at Chipola Jr. College, Winston-Salem State University, Howard University, Edison Community College, University of South Florida and George Mason University. He served in the United States Air Force, too. He has taught school in Virginia and Florida. He exhaustingly committed himself for five solid years to, finally, have T. Thomas Fortune officially honored in Jackson County. He testified for a Billy Graham crusade rally in 1986. He has done some acting in small plays, and has excellent acting talents. God mercifully spared his life from a potentially fatal motor vehicle accident in December of 1987. In 1992, he was successful at lobbying federal legislation to the floor of the United States House of Representatives. He lost a family member to random violence in 1993. In 1997, he organized an "irreversible commitment" to have Mr. Claude Neal formally recognized in Marianna. He has appeared in every major newspaper in the State of Florida, as well as several national publications, including *Jet Magazine*. As a Ronald E. McNair Fellow, in honor of the Black astronaut (Challenger), he co-authored a scientific paper in the Journal of the Society of Toxicology entitled, "Effects of Dietary Selenium (Se) and High Fat on Weight Gain; and Liver, Kidney, Colon Glutathione (GSH) of 1,2 Dimethylhydrazine Dihydrochloride (DMH) Treated Rats."

From Clinton's early childhood to his current position, he has certainly been through many dark yesterdays, but he will never give up for bright tomorrows. Once judged by some as a "troubled, problem and unproductive child", Clinton undauntingly persevered and has earned the achievement of a troubleshooting, problem-solving and productive man.

In spite of the many testing times encountered during his growth and development, he still encounters them. He has a philosophy on life and will not hesitate to tell you that it is "Never give up!!" All things considered, Clinton has no regrets and he just keeps pressing on... and that's the way it is.

Today, Clinton is single and teaches school. He has a passion for cooking and usually spends his free time reading, traveling and, of course, writing.

— WARNING —

The book you, as a Black person, are about to read is replete with powerful knowledge that is capable of causing great change... a change that has been a painfully long time coming for a people whose time has come, we as a Black people.

PART I

Essays

The Black Experience

Civil Rights

Narrative

Miscellaneous

Philosophy & Religion

Black History

A Letter

Biography

THE BLACK EXPERIENCE

Jesus Christ Was Black

Financial Fairness

Crime And Consequences

Whence We Came

Jesus Christ Was Black

"The Truth Makes ALL The Difference"

Jesus Christ was a revolutionist. His new Christianity religion taught a radically different method of reform. These doctrines subsequently caused Jesus to become a political prisoner and a martyr for His cause. Rev., Dr. Martin Luther King, Jr. is a more recent and sympathetic example. White people particularly used Jesus' teachings to develop a statement of faith for their own race.

The Holy Bible plainly describes Jesus' physical features with miraculous clarity: His hair as *"like lamb's wool"*. Woolly, kinky or curly hair is inarguably a pure African feature. *Webster's Dictionary* (3-c) specifically defines wool as "short, thick often crisp curly hair on a human head". No wonder my parents always told me that my hair was "wool", when I was a boy. Also, Revelations 2:18 clearly states *"And unto the angel of the church in Thy-a-ti'ra says: These things saith the Son of God, who hath His eyes like unto a flame of fire, and his feet are like fine brass."* Yes, Jesus Christ was Black.

In addition, in Ethiopia, where the Christian religion originated, the Ethiopians worshiped Christ as being Black. The Ethiopians also painted Jesus, the Blessed Virgin Mary and other saints in Black form.

Jesus was the Black leader of Black people suffering for complete freedom against the barbaric oppression of ruthless ruling White nations. Today, international racism is profoundly rooted in the long, long history of the deliberately deceiving passion that Jesus was a White man... with blond hair and blue eyes. Such foolish imagination is obviously historically inaccurate and precisely designed to trick Black people into believing that we are inferior to Whites. This exact tragic asininity is the very origin of global racism and White supremacy.

Incredibly stubborn, White Americans persistently propagandize a silly White Jesus right in the face of the overwhelming Biblical and historical proof that Jesus was Black and in spite of the, literally, thousands of Black Madonnas all over the world.

Jesus has an especially intimate appreciation and care for all the suffering and success of we Black people. No other people in the history of the world has endured and survived as much severe persecution, oppression, brutality and racism as we Black people and Jesus. Jesus was Black.

Jesus more personally and realistically "digs" or understands the day-to-day struggles and trials and tribulations of we Black people. Jesus went through all the pain and suffering that our ancestors went through. As slaves, we were whipped, mistreated and abused ... so was Jesus. And today, we all still experience racism, discrimination, segregation and oppression ... only because we are Black. Jesus actually feels what it is like to be Black like us.

Of course, after His resurrection, Jesus no longer has a color or race as He exists only in the omnipotent spirit, now. Nevertheless, it is an everlasting fact that Jesus physically walked this earth for 33 solid years as a Black Man and this truth makes ALL the difference.

Jesus was Black.

Financial Fairness

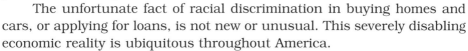

Have you ever purchased a home, automobile, business or applied for a job or loan? Chances are, you have. However, you may have paid more money, or been denied a loan or job, only because you are a minority.

The unfortunate fact of racial discrimination in buying homes and cars, or applying for loans, is not new or unusual. This severely disabling economic reality is ubiquitous throughout America.

Among the infinite forms of prevalent racial discrimination, discrimination in securing cars, homes, jobs and loans is especially damaging to minorities. Most Americans' largest financial investments lie in their cars, homes, businesses and education. Regardless of your income, obtaining these necessities is virtually impossible without a loan. However, in order to obtain a loan, one usually must have either gainful employment or some other reliable and sufficient source of income. A good credit history, as well as collateral, will also help you get your loan approved. Otherwise, obtaining these necessities is going to be difficult.

It is equally relevant to mention that some employers perform credit history checks before hiring. This is illegal; a felony. Employers do not have the right to obtain credit history information on potential employees. If you suspect or can prove that this has happened to you, the law is on your side.

Everyone needs an income and a place to live. Without transportation, it is burdensome getting to and from work (income) every day. Without work, buying a home is unreachable. African Americans' gross income averages significantly less than their White counterparts and this salary gap is consistently widening. Understandably, racial discrimination in buying a car and a home, or securing a job or loan, is particularly economically unfair to African Americans.

In addition to other forms of racial discrimination, this fundamentally deranged economic principle explains why African American families who earn identical or even greater incomes possess substantially less assets and enjoy less quality lifestyles than their White peers. This fact further explains why African American and all women employees average significantly lower salaries for identical (higher in excessive cases) job titles, with equal or greater experience and educational levels, as White male employees.

Why are minorities charged more for the exact same, sometimes inferior, products and services? It's just plain and downright discrimination. This fact is painfully true for automobile mechanical "work". Unscrupulous auto mechanics routinely overcharge minorities to the extremes. To make bad matters even worse, the mechanical parts and services are many times unnecessary or not performed. It is also true that many new and used car sales people frequently charge higher prices for identical cars for minorities and offer "bargains" to White males.

If you or someone you know suspects or can prove you paid more for a product or service only because you are a minority, immediately contact your State Commission on Agriculture and Consumer Services. You may also find relief from this agency on issues pertaining to tenant/landlord disputes.

Remember, never pay more money for anything only because you are a minority.

Crime and Consequences

According to the most recent United States' Census report, there are 270 million citizens in "America". There is a birth every 9 seconds and every 13 seconds someone dies. Among the 270 Million people in the United States, 12.2% or 32.94 million are African Americans. 72.2% or 195 million are Caucasians and 15.6% or 42.12 million are a combination of other races and ethnicities.

Within the United States' prison populations, 48% are male and female African American inmates. Forty-seven percent of the country's prison population are male and female Caucasian inmates. Florida prisons' racial statistics are one of the worst. Over sixty percent (60%) of the State Department of Correction's incarcerated are Black. This does not even include the number of African Americans who are currently on parole, probation or who have been in prison or jail. There are 16 million people in Florida. Only 15.6% or 2.5 million are African Americans!!

African American representation in Florida's prisons is more than **ten** (10) times that of Caucasian representation in Florida's prisons!!! Florida has the second highest incarceration rate in the United States. Only Texas incarcerates more people per capita than Florida. Crime and punishment is unequivocally annihilating the sacred African American marriage and family institution. Suspiciously, crime and its consequences is not affecting Whites equally.

Contrary to popular belief, these realistic demographics do not mean that Black people have a greater propensity to commit crime. Instead, it actually means that America's county, state and federal justice systems, in conjunction with educational institutions and White employers, are far less understanding and more harsh to African Americans. This fact is particularly true for Black males. Yet, justice systems are strikingly more forgiving, gentle and supportive to White criminals. This plain truth precisely explains why White criminals receive outrageously more lenient sentences and probation than Blacks who commit identical crimes or even innocent traffic infractions.

Exactly, why is this and what can we as a Black people do to correct it?

Whence We Came

During the actual beginning of humankind, there was originally only one human race present on the entire face of the earth. It was the Negroid race and, of course, present only in Africa.

Paleoanthropologist Dr. Donald Johanson's recent discovery of "LUCY" (a 3.7 million year-old female gracile [afarensis] australopithecine skeletal remain, Rowe, Bruce M. and Stein, Phillip L., *Physical Anthropology: The Core*. McGraw Hill, copyright 1995, page 245) further reconfirmed the fact that the Negroid race was the very first human race on earth. The Negro race is one of the five existing races of people.

"African American" is not a description or category of a race. Instead, it is a geographical term that merely tells where a particular person or group of people is from and where they are. For example, a Japanese who was born in Africa and relocated to America is an African American. Notwithstanding, his or her race is Oriental. "African American" is geographical. Negro is something far more profound: genetic!

The fact of the matter is, relative to "LUCY's" age, she was excavated in Hadar, Ethiopia in remarkably authentic condition. Her bones were still intact and some of her hair was still embedded in her skull. "...afarensis, the oldest and most primitive hominid (member of the family Hominidae; including humans and specifically characterized by upright bipedalism) known, was ancestral to all others (human races). The emergence of human beings began sometime after three million years ago." (Johanson, *Lucy: The Beginning of Humankind*. Simon and Schuster, pages 284-285.)

The very recent discovery of a strikingly similar hominid (human forerunner) fossil in the Sterkfontein caves near South Africa is dated between 3.6 and 3.2 million years before present. The dating in South Africa is done by bio-correlations with fossils that are radiometrically dated in East Africa, where "radio datable" deposits are used. This simply means that the freshly discovered Sterkfontein skeleton is less primitive than "LUCY".

As time lapsed after "LUCY" died, aboriginal Africans began to migrate out of Africa to other parts of the world... including Europe. Negro migration out of Africa was impaired by the continental shift, due to wider ocean barriers.

As the aboriginal Africans migrated to Europe in particular, the colder climate, decreased sunlight and changes in food sources caused the first Europeans' (Negroes) dermal (skin) tissue and iris melanin (pigmentation), as well as certain other anatomical physiologies, to evolve for strict survival purposes.

For example, compared to any place in Africa, the climate in Europe is significantly colder and drier, and their is less sunlight. In order to compensate for these deficiencies, the aboriginal Africans who migrated to Europe evolved longer noses, with more membrane exposure. This newly developed anatomical feature allowed increased inhalation of warmer and more moist air. Also, decreased pigmentation in the first Europeans' skin facilitated sun ray exposure and absorption. This perfectly explains why Caucasians sunburn easily and acclimate more efficiently to cold weather while the exact reciprocal is true for Negroes.

Marked dietary changes also caused early Europeans' lips to undergo atrophy (become smaller). It is also a fact that the reason many Negroes today are lactose intolerant is because cow milk was not a part of the early African diet. The first African settlers of Europe began to milk cows and evolved the necessary enzyme (lactase) to digest its sugar, lactose. For this reason, Caucasians can digest nearly all dairy products. There is an interesting explanation for the sickle cell anemia trait and disease, as well as any other inheritable disease, predominance in the world Negro population.

Among the five races of subhuman species in the world today, the most distinct physiological and anatomical differences exist between the Negro and the Caucasian. This fact is especially true for the marrow stem cells (center of bones where blood cells are produced) of these two races. Because Black people and White people differ more than any other two races, this partly explains why the greatest racism exists between these two races than any others.

Racism is actually ignorance. It is a personal and emotionally acquired attitude. No evidence exists to even suggest, let alone prove, that racism is genetically inherited. However, it is certain that, like all other personal attitudes and deportment, racism is definitely learned. This also explains why racist mentalities are virtually nonexistent in young children and the elderly. It seems as though these particular two groups of people have no consciousness or care for skin color. They only want to play with or be cared for by whoever is willing.

More than any other single factor in the history of the world, racism has cost our global society the most: incalculable amounts of money and literally millions of human lives... mostly by way of war, slavery or other forms of racial intolerance. Although over three-fourths of the world's seven billion people are "colored", Negroes specifically have always been the main target of racism in predominant "White America".

The Most Segregated City In The South

According to Reynolds Farley, Vice-President of the Russell Sage Foundation in New York, Lee County (Fort Myers), Florida is the most segregated metropolitan area of the United States. This fact was determined by examining data from the Census of 1990 PL-171 file showing the distribution of Whites and Blacks by block groups.

Today, segregation, in and of itself, is purely an issue of personal choice and racial preference. Essentially, segregation is inevitable and irrelevant.

Realistically, most White people do not want to live in Black neighborhoods nor do White parents wish to send their children to schools having high Black student and teacher populations. In fact, for many White Ft. Myers residents, it is more than enough merely working with Blacks at their jobs. So they live, worship, shop and play as far away as they can get from Blacks after work and on the weekends. As far as Ft. Myers Blacks are concerned, surely they would love to work in the highest paying jobs, live in the more excellent neighborhoods, send their children to the "better" schools and enjoy their entertainment at some of the more elegant scenes in Ft. Myers.... and they can!

There is absolutely no one or no law in this land that says Black people cannot enjoy the same elegant lifestyles that their White counterparts enjoy. President Johnson's signing of the June 29, 1964 civil rights bill makes this fact miraculously clear. Make no mistake about it though, there are Ft. Myers Blacks who unapologetically exercise their civil rights, reject the concept of segregation and leisurely enjoy more elegant lifestyles than many of their economically comparable White peers. This is their own choice. But most Ft. Myers Blacks personally choose to live, worship and play in their own Black communities, in spite of the fact that they clearly have the ways and means to do otherwise. Black communities in Ft. Myers were founded on the history of a previous Black community, church or individuals.

This is the reason segregation is both inevitable and irrelevant.

Segregation is a natural and personal choice. If you do not like asparagus, naturally, you are not going to eat it. If you don't like something or someone, nothing on the face of this earth can force you to change your personal preferences. Simply put, if you do not like living around Black or White people, as long as your money can back you up, you are not going to do it, even though it is perfectly legal and you are protected under the United States Constitution.

Instead of following the segregation scapegoat, it is far more wise for Blacks and Whites to face the disgraceful reality of discrimination and inequality in Ft. Myers. Segregation and discrimination are mutually exclusive factors; however, they are best friends... when you see one, the other is near. Segregation is, understandably, unheard of in Black communities. Segregation and discrimination invariably raise their pathetic heads where Black people are a minority. This fact is ubiquitously applicable.

Segregation alone is acceptable. When considering the best interests of we Black people, I can easily prove numerous examples where segregation is inarguably beneficial, most notably in the public school system. Notwithstanding, discrimination and inequality is indisputably illegal, unconstitutional and sinful yesterday, today and tomorrow, and it ought to be immediately rejected by both Blacks and Whites everywhere and every time.

A very unfortunate site it is to see the people of Ft. Myers being mislead and alarmed over segregation, especially after all these years. As segregated as Ft. Myers may actually be, the fair *"City of Palms"* is now more integrated than it has ever been in its history. The most segregated time and place in the entire United States is 11:00 a.m. on Sunday... Ft. Myers is no exception. Paradoxically, the churches are the most segregated sites in every city, yet this routine reality has never been made into a national racial issue. Why?

Originally, every city in the United States was completely segregated. Slavery, of course, was the initial cause of American segregated communities... in the North as well as the South. After the Civil War, segregation was severely reconfirmed by the atrociously violent Ku Klux Klan. Stringent Jim Crow laws sealed up any breathing room for integration that the Klan may have left behind.

Supreme Court Justices and Presidents Eisenhower and Johnson did not make segregation unconstitutional. Hundreds of thousands of conscious Black men, women and young children who knowingly risked their lives by participating in dangerous sit-ins, protests, boycotts, freedom rides and street demonstrations forced segregation to become unconstitutional!!! Fed-up Black citizens in Jacksonville, Tallahassee, Birmingham, Selma and Montgomery were literally bludgeoned to death in the dirty streets by hateful White mobs and derelict law enforcement officers... all in the name of integration and racial equality!!!

Why should segregation in Ft. Myers abruptly become such an alarming issue now? To make matters even worse, Lee County's White elected officials and constituents laughed at and blatantly ignored the United States Supreme Court's May 31, 1955 "all deliberate speed" public schools integration order. Incredibly bullheaded, not until the federal government much later forced the Lee County School Board to initiate bussing and pry open its all White schools to Black student integration did segregation finally begin to fragment in Lee County. Today, parents are allowed to personally choose the schools they wish for their children to attend in Lee County.

Where Is "America"?

It is paradoxically ironic that Native Americans and African Americans, the only two people of great might who actually suffered the most discrimination and oppression by White America and all levels of American government, still to this very moment suffer the worst racial discrimination and most horrific oppression by the historical g.o.b.n. (goooooooooood ol' boys network).

The disgraceful reality of American history glaringly shows that Native Americans were pitilessly raped and robbed of their native land and natural resources, and literally died by the hundreds and hundreds of thousands in genuine commitment to protect it from the outrageously wicked intrusion of the European settlers. This murderous intrusion originated at Christopher Columbus' ruthless killings of scores of Native American tribes when he accidentally sailed to America in 1492. Native Americans' life-sustaining bison were barbarically slaughtered by the White man to near tragic extinction as well.

Even worse, during the delirious California Gold Rush of 1848, the White man barbarically murdered thousands upon thousands of Native Americans just for fun because they were in the way of "their" gold. It is an equally urgent fact that Native Americans officially recognize Thanksgiving as "a day of mourning", because of the manner in which the Pilgrims (1620) betrayed and abused them.

Today, in "America", virtually all Native Americans remain dumped and totally derelict on federal reservations, in despicable condition, scattered across the country. Native Americans account for less than one percent (1%) of the current United States population! White Americans take up 72.2% of the US population!! What do you think about this?!!!

The absolute realness of the infinite moral blemishes of American history shamefully shows further that millions of native Africans were brutally forced into America as slave property by money-hungry and immoral Caucasians who had been kicked out of England! And these most peaceful, friendly and gentle Africans were not brought to

America for any dandy vacation or pleasure touring, but rather for dragging into the unimaginably inhumane, cremating furnace of the graphic indignities of the American slave trade system!! Routine lynchings and burnings of African American men, women and children by armies of White cowards, usually commanded by the county sheriff, are merely a fraction of the numerous, unspeakably disgusting realities!!! And these outright anti-Christ introductions of our African ancestors to America in 1619 commenced the absolute, categorically, demonic racism and relentless oppression which persistently endures as a fierce plague to all African Americans here and now!!

Today, like Native Americans, African Americans perpetually suffer the bottom ebb of poverty, hopelessly failed equal educational opportunities, deplorable housing, out-of-control employment/loan discrimination and pathetically inept representation in local, state and national governmental affairs and judicial proceedings. What percentage do African Americans make up of the entire US population?

Only you, as a unique individual, are the one who can find "America". Care and education is the map.

Where To Go From Here

The African American institution remains to this very day affected by the nearly 400 years of unyielding and worsening racial discrimination and pure oppression in the United States. This discrimination and oppression originated in every conceivable way for the Negro even before his arrival to the Americas in 1619. Initiating in education, employment, economics, housing, judiciary and politics, defacto discrimination and blatant oppression by Whites on African Americans endures furiously here and now!

Still the African American's true and most urgent priority, this perpetual and powerful discrimination is pitifully manifested as Black-on-Black crime. Today's African American is completely fed up from being refused equitable and quality education only because he or she is an African American. Today's African American is fed up from being repeatedly withheld sufficient and promotional employment only because you are an African American. This fact is especially true when you see the same White people working next to you at the job receiving promotions and raises, and enjoying elegant lifestyles at home. When you are repeatedly denied a loan to better the quality of your lifestyle and are forced to mortgage your home to secure your debtors, you become fed up. When you are repeatedly declined safe and affordable housing for your family only because you are an African American, you become fed up. When you are repeatedly teased with your dignity by the police and court systems only because you are an African American, you become fed up. When you are repeatedly rejected political fairness and proper representation in local, state, and the federal government only because you are an African American, you become fed up.

What should you African Americans do when you are mistreated like this? Get an education, or get more education, African American brothers and sisters! Rely only on yourself. Education... it is the only way. Never give up!!!

NARRATIVE ESSAY

— SPECIAL OCCASION WITH LaSALLE D. LEFFALL, JR., M.D. —

My Special Observance of
Dr. Leffall's Return to FAMU

(A Centennial Celebration Event)

My Special Observance of Dr. Leffall's Return to FAMU

A Centennial Celebration Event

It is Friday, October 2, 1987, at exactly 9:25 am. I am eagerly sitting on a concrete bench directly in front of the water fountain of FAMU's Quadrangle, scanning the in-marching scholars. These particular individuals are orderly proceeding to their designated seats for the prompt commencement of the Florida Agricultural and Mechanical University Centennial Convocation. After briefly scanning the marching scholars, I quickly sight the person I was hoping to greet, LaSalle D. Leffall, Jr., M.D. ... *my role model.*

Moments before Dr. Leffall reaches the wooden platform and takes his reserved seat, I nimbly run to a vacant seat that is anterior to him. Good. I now have a more excellent panoramic view of the entire convocation activity. Everything is now set and prepared to begin. It is 9:30 am and the convocation is officially initiated by the prelude *"Blessed Are They"*; University Marching "100" Band.

... Time has lapsed. Dr. Leffall has just completed his eloquent key note speech and he is now being awarded the honorary degree of Doctorate of Science. Having freshly received his latest diploma, Dr. Leffall stood with perfect dignity as he accepted a full four (4) minute applause from the roused audience. It was now 11:43 am.

The convocation was now concluding and the platform guests were preparing to gracefully proceed to the Perry-Paige Building. I then inconspicuously crossed Dr. Leffall's path and most humbly sat on the opposite side of the walkway, near Dr. Foote.

Dr. Foote (now deceased) is an equally significant physician as the Maryland native was the actual attending doctor who delivered Dr. Leffall on May 22, 1930, at the FAMU Hospital.

At this time, Dr. Leffall was approaching Dr. Foote and me. As he passed us, I immediately stood erect and proudly provided the internationally acclaimed surgeon with an especially warm smile and firm handshake, without interfering with his orderly march.

After the marching scholars freed themselves from the large crowd, I leisurely assisted Dr. Foote to his automobile. Upon seeing to his secure departure, I briskly walked to the Perry-Paige Building. When I arrived, I could only see Dr. Leffall's head as he was surrounded by a countless number of family, friends, visitors, faculty, staff, students, former schoolmates, photographers, journalists, strangers and mere curious spectators. Even one hour later, there were still more fans, admirers and friends crying, amazed and asking for Dr. Leffall's autograph. I was also very pleased to have had the opportunity to meet Dr. Leffall's sister and mother (now deceased).

It was now rapidly approaching 1:00 pm and everything was "operating" just splendidly. Dr. Leffall was literally speaking to two people and signing his autograph simultaneously. If he wasn't meeting old friends and former classmates, or signing autographs, he was having his photograph taken.

Lunch was now being served, but it seemed nearly impossible for Dr. Leffall to obtain a simple opportunity to sit down and enjoy his fruitful meal. Finally, when he did get a chance, he was persistently interrupted as even more and more old friends, guests and even perfect strangers greeted a down-to-earth Dr. Leffall, at his meal table.

It was now 1:30 pm and an exhausted Dr. Leffall was being greeted by yet more family, friends, loved ones and classmates as he simultaneously navigated his way towards his chauffeur's vehicle to depart. However, just before he left, he told me that he would see me at the unveiling of the distinguished FAMU Graduate Gallery at 3:00 pm.

It was now 3:00 pm. Dr. Leffall was on the second floor of FAMU's Tucker Hall. He is present for the unveiling of the distinguished graduates of the College of Arts and Sciences of Florida A & M University. At this particular time, it was more crowded than previously at Perry-Paige. At the conclusion of this program, Dr. Leffall sped away with an escort, in an apparent effort to avoid the crowd. Little did I know that I would again meet him at 11:00 pm on that very night. It was now 5:16 pm.

It is 11:00 pm. Dr. Leffall is inside Florida A & M University's Grand Ballroom, attending a one-hundred dollar dinner. With less than ten cents in my pocket, inappropriate clothing for the occasion, and determination, I assumed a waiter and began to make my way to him. Knowing that I had to have some type of food or beverage to get to Dr. Leffall's dinner table, I found my way to the kitchen and obtained a pitcher of water. I then waitered myself back to Dr. Leffall's table and asked him if I could serve him some water. Dr. Leffall was speaking to another individual at his table when I asked him for the water serving. Without looking at me, he said "No thanks," and continued his conversation. By this time, FAMU's President (Dr. Frederick S. Humphries), who was dining with Dr. Leffall, was becoming noticeably suspicious, so I knew I had to act fast. I asked Dr. Leffall in a rather raised voice, "Is everything lovely respected sir?" At that moment, Dr. Leffall immediately turned around and recognized me. He also informed Dr. Humphries of our previous meeting in the District of Columbia.

It was now rapidly approaching midnight. Dr. Leffall informed me that he would speak to me at a later time.

At the conclusion of Dr. Leffall's meal and the centennial banquet, I escorted the stately surgeon, as well as his mother and sister, to the exterior of the building. Gradually, Dr. Leffall made his way to one of the FAMU officer's patrol automobiles. I then presented a "good night" to the famous physician and his family, and informed him that I would see them at tomorrow's football game. It was now 11:45 pm.

Immediately after departing the prestigious surgeon, I walked back to my Sampson Hall dormitory and began to contemplate, heavily. I was trying to determine what would be the most appropriate gift to present to the remarkable medical scientist as a souvenir. After much hard and careful consideration, I finally decided to prepare a small booklet of my own scientific and research accomplishments. After I completed the souvenir, I placed the booklet on my desk and went to bed. As I lay in my bed that night, I wondered... I wondered if the illustrious oncologist would accept my only offer. It was 2:30 am.

Today is Saturday, October 3, at 6:30 am. Although the FAMU football game does not officially begin until another seven hours, I have proceeded to Famu's Bragg Stadium with my *Hyman's Comparative Anatomy* textbook and Dr. Leffall's souvenir tucked firmly under my right arm.

At 1:25 pm I found my way to the president's guest room of the pressbox. One particular lady whom is also present has asked me what am I doing here. I explained to the woman that I wish to see Dr. Leffall and present to him my prepared souvenir. I asked the lady to please allow me to stay until he arrives.

It is now 1:32 pm and Dr. Leffall is just arriving. I speak to him and shake his hand, firmly. I then ask him what time was he going to leave and he told me "After the game, and then I'm going to Reverend Miles' home." After the unidentified woman heard Dr. Leffall tell me this, she asked me to remove myself from the president's guest room. I replied to the lady by saying "Very good 'mam... thank you so kindly." I then quietly walked out of the room with my *Comparative Anatomy* book, and Dr. Leffall's prepared souvenir, tucked gently against my right serratus anterior.

I was now outside and beginning to wonder how I could get back into the president's guest room to present my organized souvenir to Dr. Leffall. Suddenly, I saw Mr. Jackson and kindly asked him to please notify Dr. Leffall that I've prepared a souvenir for him, and I wished to present it to him. Mr. Jackson asked me to stay where I was while he generously proceeded to summon the friendly surgeon. Less than five minutes I waited, and then I saw Dr. Leffall and Mr. Jackson exit the guest room.

I spoke to Dr. Leffall again and asked him to permit me to present the prepared souvenir to him. Dr. Leffall responded, "Very good, Clinton." I then asked the expert oncologist to please keep the souvenir... for it was from my heart. Dr. Leffall glanced over the souvenir and then paused to ask for my grades and the courses I was currently taking. I revealed this information to the prodigious surgeon and he told me to continue to work hard.

Dr. Leffall took my *Comparative Anatomy* textbook and scanned it until something in the book grasped his attention. I then explained to him that I was preparing for the dissection of the adult feline on Tuesday.

Peculiarly, Dr. Leffall firmly shook my right hand for a final time and, with an enchanting smile, encouraged me to remember all the advice that he'd given me. Barely, I told Dr. Leffall, "Very good... sir, I definitely will... do that." He then said, "Okay Clinton, I'll be looking forward to hearing from you." At that, my role model re-entered the president's guest room.

Hesitantly, I turned away from the door and walked the long journey back to my Sampson Hall dormitory. It was now 2:00 pm.

MISCELLANEOUS

The Viewing of Halley's Comet

Chrono

Let's Face It

The Viewing of Halley's Comet

— April 26, 1986 —

It was 1:30 Saturday morning. My telescope and accessories were gently tucked under my left arm as I rode the elevator to Florida A & M University's observatory. When I reached the fifth floor, I climbed up the ladder to the University's observatory. About halfway up the ladder, I saw about thirty people, all making diligent efforts to view Halley's Comet. For many, it would be their only view. Dr. William P. Tucker, one of the FAMU's physics professors, arranged five telescopes and binoculars for the viewers. When I reached the roof, where the observatory was located, everyone seemed to stop viewing Halley's Comet and focused their comet-hungry eyes upon me. Feeling a bit uncomfortable, I acted as though I was not there. Soon, everyone went back to viewing the comet. I could not clearly see any faces because my eyes hadn't acclimated to the darkness.

When I obtained a stable position on the creviced roof, I could hear many people talking with a great deal of excitement. I could even hear babies crying and children cheerfully explaining to their parents what they saw through the telescopes and binoculars. I saw fathers holding their small children up to the large telescopes to view Halley's Comet, for the first time. Some of the children were so young they may live to see Halley's Comet again, in 2061. Also, I could hear elderly men stating they could see nothing through the telescopes, which were focused directly on the fuzzy snowball (Halley's Comet). Perhaps their old age had prohibited their viewing of Halley's Comet for a second time. Some viewers complained they saw nothing through the powerful telescopes. Dr. Tucker worked diligently to assemble the telescopes for the convenience of the viewers. They just seemed to have no appreciation for their views of the comet. It made me feel bad because they were so unthankful for what they did see. Nevertheless, I heard some viewers express their appreciation to others for their viewing of Halley's Comet. One viewer stated "Well, it's better than seeing nothing at all."

By now, it was 1:55 am. Dr. Tucker was almost at three places at the same time, trying to assist his guests to view Halley's Comet. I said to myself, "I wish I could assist him."

Soon, Dr. Tucker noticed I had my personal telescope and provided me with illumination to assemble it. He gave me a flashlight and suggested that I go inside the observatory, where I would have more room. After I assembled my telescope, I asked Dr. Tucker where could I stand it to view the comet. I had never viewed Halley's Comet through my own telescope before and I was anxious to do so. Professor Tucker suggested that I step out onto an adjacent roof. He strongly insisted that I be very careful because this particular area was not fenced in. I told Professor Tucker "okay", and he went with me on the adjacent roof to focus my telescope.

It now was 2:06 am, one of the most exciting moments of my eighteen years of life. Professor Tucker maneuvered my telescope for about 40 seconds and then pinpointed the comet in the center of my telescope. He then said, "okay, I've got it... go ahead and take a look." Immediately I looked into my telescope and saw the comet. I was very happy and excited at this special occasion. I stared for about 10 minutes into my telescope, contemplating Halley's Comet. I was aware that my chances of ever seeing it again were slim. I loved what I saw and I appreciated it.

It was now approximately 2:25 am. I left the adjacent roof and joined the other viewers in the observatory. I also saw the planet Saturn through one of the telescopes that Professor Tucker had on display. It was the most beautiful planet I'd ever seen.

For about another hour I went from telescope to telescope and binocular to binocular, viewing Halley's Comet. By this time, most of the viewers had returned home with a thought and a view in their minds that they would probably die with. It was a very special moment to me. Meanwhile, my telescope remained on the adjacent roof, staring at Halley's Comet, where I left it. I then carefully walked out on the roof and looked at the comet for a final time for the night. I picked up my telescope and took it back inside the observatory to disassemble it. I then reluctantly walked out of the observatory. As I approached the ladder, I turned around and told Professor Tucker that I was preparing to depart, and I really appreciated his assistance. He said "okay", and I told him I would see him later. Slowly and cautiously, I climbed down the ladder to catch the elevator to the second floor of Jones Hall... and walked back to my Gibbs Hall dormitory.

As I walked away from the building, with my telescope and its accessories tucked firmly under my left arm, I thought of the fuzzy snowball (over 39 million miles away) that I had just viewed through my telescope. Then, I wondered. I wondered if I would ever see Halley's Comet again. It was 3:45 am.

Chrono

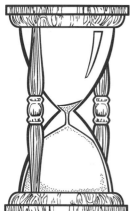

What is the most absolute necessity in all the world and the universe?

No human being can sense or detect it: You cannot see it. You cannot smell it. You cannot touch it. You cannot taste it. You cannot hear it.

Everything needs it. Even light, the fastest phenomenon known, takes it. Everyone alive has some of it. It is immeasurably valuable, but some people unwisely waste it. It has no beginning nor an end. However, when you die, you run out of it. It is what schedules, tables and deadlines are strictly made on. It can be desperately constraining and, therefore, a lack of it is capable of causing great stress. No rate of speed could ever stand a chance of challenging it. If lost, it can never be made up. It is crucial to sleep. It is relative.

It does not stop, wait or change. It is perfectly constant. We use chronometers and calendars to measure it, but it can never be controlled. It is not for sale. It made the past, is the present and determines the future. Presidents, billionaires, physicians, queens, and everyone in between, must bow to it. It is unimaginably powerful. It changes all things and it tells.

What is it? Think about it.... *take your time.*

Let's Face It

Let's face it, all those who are fertile are not fit to be parents. If a child grows up to be a bad adult, he or she had no parents or bad parents.

Want to drive? You need a license. Cut hair? You still need a license. The same requirements apply even if you want to fish or hunt. However, if you want to have children, have them! The sky is the limit. The law does not stipulate that you have permission to be a parent.

Think about all the children who's lives and limbs, literally and figuratively speaking, would be saved if irresponsible and negligent people were prohibited from having children by an effective "parenting licensing" agency.

I say let's do away with the overwhelmed reactive Department of Children and Families, and replace it with a proactive and efficient "parenting licensing" agency. Exactly where is the logic when it is unlawful to do manicures without a license, but it is perfectly permissible for abusive people to freely have children?

PHILOSOPHY AND RELIGION

Merry Christmas?

Life After Death Exists

Merry Christmas?

What does Christmas actually mean? Who originated Christmas? Where did Christmas begin? Why did Christmas begin? When did Christmas begin? How did Christmas begin? Who really is Santa Claus and how did he get involved in Christmas? When was Jesus actually born and what does He have to do with Christmas?

The Black Jesus Christ may have been born in the late summer or early fall of 12 B.C. and the star (North Star) that lead the three Wise Men to Bethlehem was actually Halley's Comet. As a matter of fact, Halley's Comet appeared over the Middle East in 12 B.C., showing up at latitude 31º N. Latitude 31ºN is the latitude of Bethlehem!

Edmund Halley was an English astronomer who accurately predicted the appearance of the comet, twice, even though he did not live to witness its second appearance. Halley noticed from his astronomy records that the comet he was observing appeared immutably every previous 76 years. Therefore, it is perfectly logical, as evidenced by simple mathematics, that this same comet appeared during 12 B.C.

The traditional December 25th birth date is misleading because of the reference in Luke (second chapter, verses 8-12) to shepherds in the fields near Bethlehem as the first to learn a new King had been born. Shepherds' flocks were not allowed in the fields after they were plowed in October or November so that winter rains could soak into the parched grounds. However, shepherds were allowed to graze their sheep in late summer and early fall to eat the stubble of crops and fertilize the fields. According to these facts, it is highly likely that Jesus was born sometime between late July and early October of 12 B.C.

The Star of Bethlehem was an early visitation of Halley's Comet. Halley's Comet returns near earth every seventy-six years. Thus, the comet was visible in 12 B.C. According to the book of Matthew, second chapter, second verse, the three Wise Men were guided to the birth site of Jesus by the North Star. Moreover, the book of Matthew states that the three Wise Men visualized the North Star twice. This fact clearly correlates with the appearance of Halley's Comet. The three Wise Men's impression that the star pointed the way to Bethlehem might have come from the tail of the comet, which is some billions of miles long.

Some scholars who researched the birth date of Jesus concluded that He was born in 1 A.D. There is even a reference in the book of Matthew of the Bible that states "King Herod was still alive at the time of Jesus' birth." Herod, the King of Judae, is believed to have died in 4 B.C. Furthermore, scholars have very recently discovered that the census that the Book of Luke said brought Mary and Joseph to Bethlehem probably was carried out while Quinrinis was governor.

Christmas is actually derived from the Old English Cristes Maesse (Christ's Mass). In German this festival is called Weichnacht, meaning Holy Night. In Latin the feast is Dies natis Domini. In Italian, Natale. Spanish, La Navidad. Christmas is Noel in French and it probably came from the Latin, natlis. Yule comes into modern English from the Anglo Saxon geol, a feast of the winter solstice. The Epiphany (Twelfth Day or Little Christmas) commemorates the baptism of Jesus, the visit of the three Wise Men to Bethlehem and the miracle of Cana. Twelfth night is the Epiphany's eve which is celebrated on January 6. Christmas is also known as the feast of the nativity of Jesus Christ. Easter, Pentecost and the Epiphany out rank Christmas in liturgical importance.

The Christians of Egypt began celebrating Christmas as early as 200 A.D. The Egyptians celebrated Christ's birthday on January 6, as members of the Eastern Orthodox church do. The Saturnalia, a Roman religious festival of Saturn, was originally held on December 17. The Church of Rome, nonetheless, eventually extended the Saturnalia to December 25. Furthermore, in 353 A.D., Bishop Liberius ordered every person in his lands to celebrate Jesus' birthday on December 25. Bishop Liberius assigned this particular date for Christmas because the Romans already celebrated the Feast of Saturn (Saturnalia) and the Mithraic feast of the sun-god (Nutalis solis invicti) on this day. Moreover, the Church of Rome wanted to turn the people away from the pagan observance of the winter solstice to a day of exclusive honor for Jesus.

One may have noticed or perhaps written the word Christmas as "Xmas". The form of the name originated in the early Christian church. In Greek, "X" is the first letter of Jesus Christ's name. It was most usually utilized as a very Holy symbol. Jesus (Joshua) means "Savior". Christ means "Anointed", in Greek.

For most of the past, people have observed Christmas as a religious festival. However, they gradually adopted more customs unrelated to the church. In England, during the Middle Ages, Christmas became the happiest day of the year. Celebrations consequently became so rowdy that the Puritans in England did away with the observance of Christmas by law in 1633, and the colonist in New England copied the English laws. The blue laws of the Massachusetts Bay and New Haven colonies even outlawed mince pies. Nevertheless, immigrants brought with them Christmas customs from many lands.

The idea of a Santa Claus originated in Germany and became widespread in the 19th century. His original name was Saint Nicholas, which was adopted as Santa Claus. Literally, Santa Claus comes from the word satan. The original "Santa" was, indeed, evil and satan-like, thus Santa. This should come as no surprise. The original Santa (satan) was actually a thief... breaking into homes at night and taking articles from the homes and stuffing them in his characteristic sack. The idea that Santa enter homes at night through the chimney stems from the fact that most early German homes had chimneys and Santa intruded into the homes to burglarize them by this specific method. The added idea that Santa has crafty elves comes from the fact that the original German Santa exploited child-labor to perform his satanic deeds.

Today, the proposed idea of a Santa Claus and his association with Christmas has been heavily accepted and capitalized upon. The entire world, especially in America, has made the Christmas and Santa Claus combination into a multi-trillion dollar month (December) of marketing and selling products, services and celebrations. Most Christmas advertisements and announcements begin in October; however, many profit-seekers and pagan worshippers begin Christmas as early as September or even August. Christmas itself is clearly a European-originated holiday. And like most other man-made holidays, Christmas strategically has far more economical significance than it does any religious significance.

Stress, depression and crime also appear at record levels during the Christmas holidays as a result of our heavily materialistic American society intensely emphasizing that everyone should get everything they want, go where they want, do what they want, be with their family and friends and simply be happy during the holidays. This, unfortunately, is not realistic for most people and these distant expectations cause great feelings of inadequacy at this time of the year.

Insofar as what Christmas has to do with Jesus is concerned, the answer is nothing. Most people who celebrate Christmas usually attempt to force a religious or Biblical significance to the holiday. But among the hundreds of thousands of words in the Bible, not one of them is Christmas. Jesus nor God instructed man to celebrate His (Jesus') birthday as He did His death, which is in the form of Passover. Even if God had instructed man to celebrate Jesus' birthday as Christmas, we would still fail because Santa (satan) and the wild frenzy of buying and selling would trample any realization of Jesus.

Life After Death Exists

Life after death really does exist. Read it yourself, in the Bible:

- "For we know that if our earthly house of this tabernacle were dissolved, we have a building of God, a house not made with hands, eternal in the heavens." (II Cor. 5:1)
- "And God shall wipe away all tears from their eyes; and there shall be no more death, neither sorrow, nor crying, neither shall there be any more pain: for the former things are passed away." (Rev. 21:4)
- "And I saw the dead, small and great, stand before God; and the books were opened: and another book was opened, which is the book of life: and the dead were judged out of those things which were written in the books, according to their works." (Rev. 20:2)
- "If a man dies, shall he live again? All the days... I will wait, till my change comes. You shall call, and I will answer You; You shall desire the work of Your hands." (Job 14:4-15, New King James)
- "Concerning His son Jesus Christ our Lord, which was made of the seed of David according to the flesh; And declared to be the Son of God with power, according to the spirit of holiness, by the resurrection from the dead." (Rom. 1:3-4)
- "For as in Adam all die, even so in Christ shall all be made alive. But each one in his own order." (I Cor. 15:22-23, New King James)
- "Blessed and holy is he that part in the first resurrection: on such the second death hath no power, but they shall be priests of God, and shall reign with him a thousand years." (Rev. 20:6)
- "There is a spirit in man." (Job 32:8)
- "The spirit shall return unto God who gave it." (Eccl. 12:7)
- The day we die, our "thoughts perish". (Ps. 146:4)
- "The dead know nothing." (Eccl. 9:5, New King James)
- Man was created a "living soul". (Gen 2:7)
- "Marvel not at this: for the hour is coming, in which all that are in the graves shall hear His voice." (John 5:28)
- "I am He that liveth, and was dead; and, behold, I am alive for evermore. Amen; and have the keys of hell and of death." (Rev. 1:18)

BLACK HISTORY

African Americans of Distinction

African Americans of Distinction

Remarkable achievements and phenomenal contributions by mighty African Americans are endless! Unfortunately, most are unrealized or other people undeservingly receive their credit. Since Black History is, unjustly, not taught in most public schools, few people ever become aware of the many, many unique and extraordinary achievements and contributions Black people have made to the world-at-large.

Ironically, however the unfortunate, more White people study and are more knowledgeable of Black History than we Blacks. Why?

Most people probably know something about Booker T. Washington and W.E.B. Du Bois, but did you know that T. Thomas Fortune was an equally effective Black leader?

Did you know that the Honorable Shirley Chisholm was the first African American to make a major campaign for the presidency? Did you know that there were five (5) mulatto US Presidents? Did you know that Ancient African Imhotep is the real Father of Medicine? Did you also know that Thomas Jefferson, third president of "America", fathered a large number of children by a young African slave named Sally Hemmings? Beethoven, the greatest musician in the history of the world, was a "dark mulatto". The hush puppy (cornmeal fritter) was actually invented by an African American family while fishing at Lake Jackson in Tallahassee. L.R. Johnson designed the bicycle in 1899. A.C. Richard designed and constructed the Coca-Cola bottle. Matthew Henson was the first man to plant the American Flag at the North Pole. Ralph Johnson Bunche was the first African American to achieve the Nobel Peace Prize in 1950. Air Force Colonel Frederick Drew Gregory was the first African American to pilot a space shuttle mission. Col. Gregory is the nephew of Dr. Charles Richard Drew! What were the circumstances of Dr. Drew's death?

The achievements and contributions African Americans have made to the world are infinite and invaluable.

For years now, school children all over "America" have been conditioned with the same stories about the same Black people... if they've been told at all. Why is it a shock that other Black greats in numerous fields of endeavor (medicine, politics, science, technology, math, literature, business, finance, etc.) have made tremendous achievements and contributions ... only to be ignored or other undeserving people have received their credit?

I once had an history professor at FAMU who could instantly name a greater Black when arbitrarily given any White person of noted acclaim. For example, if you were to tell him Thomas Edison, he would immediately tell you Granville T. Woods. Or if you say Lawton Chiles, he would promptly say Governor P.B.S. Pinchback. Even if you were to say Albert Einstein, he would without hesitation say the great genius Benjamin Banneker.

Professor was so amazingly knowledgeable of Black History, he systematically stunned hundreds of students by effortlessly naming distinguished African Americans from each and every one of their home towns... no matter how large or how small (from Los Angeles to Marianna)!

All young people need dignified role models, but this need is especially desperate for African American children. Role models can come from both the past and present, and should come from all areas, not just science or sports or civil rights. We mighty Black people literally built this country!

Black hands that once picked cotton in the Mississippi Delta today program computers in Silicon Valley! Children who once instinctively dodged aimless bullets in the South Bronx today save lives and heal the sick in Wyoming with their expert medical knowledge and technological skills!! Black scholars today teach at the very colleges and universities where they were once denied admission to learn!!!

Black people have contributed enormously to virtually every aspect of life, and their contributions deserve far more than the abbreviated attention they may receive during Black History Month in February.

Did you know?...

Leotyne Price

Leotyne Price sang the leading role in "Antony and Cleopatra" when the new Metropolitan Opera House opened September 16, 1966. Miss Price, referred to as the "voice of the century" and the "girl with the golden voice", was born in Mississippi. Paul Robeson, who contributed to her training, gave benefit concerts for Miss Price. Leotyne Price was the first Black star in an opera on television when she performed "Tosca" in 1955.

Norbert Rillieux

The intelligence of slave-born Norbert Rillieux was recognized at an early age and he was sent to Paris for education, staying on for a time as instructor. He published several papers on the steam engine and steam economy. He returned to Louisiana and accepted the task of reorganizing a sugar refining plant. Sugar cane juice at that time was made into sugar by a slow, costly process. Rillieux developed a process which reduced costs and produced a superior quality of sugar. The process was successfully adopted in South Florida, Cuba and Mexico. It was also used in other industries which had the problem of liquid reduction.

Benjamin Banneker

Benjamin Banneker, a literal genius, was a master of mathematics, astronomy, architecture, agriculture and invention. He designed the blueprints for the White House, US Capitol, Treasury Department, plus other federal buildings ... all by photographic memory!

The original designer got into a dispute with members of the surveying team and angrily took the only existing blueprints with him to France. President George Washington (who was a regular grower and user of cannabis) was worried, and so called on Benjamin Banneker. Banneker had only seen the blueprints once! Washington, DC, with its great avenues and buildings, stands today as a monument to Banneker's miraculous ingenuity.

Banneker's preoccupation with science in no way diminished his concern for the plight of Blacks. In a twelve-page letter to Thomas Jefferson (the same man who became famous for hypocritically saying "All men are created equal"), Banneker flatly rejected his statement that "Blacks are inferior to Whites". Banneker, himself, was living proof that the strength of the mind is in no way connected to the color of the skin. Living four years longer than he predicted, Banneker died on Saturday, October 25, 1806.

The "Virginia Calculator"

In the 1700's, a slave named Tom Fuller was born in Virginia. Like most slaves, Mr. Fuller was completely illiterate as it was illegal to educate slaves. He could not even tell one written number from the other. However, he could quickly tell you that there are 31,536,000 seconds in a year! Mr. Fuller could immediately tell you that a person who is 70 years, 17 days and 12 hours old has lived exactly 2,210,500,800 (2 billion, 210 million, 500 hundred thousand and 800) seconds!! Mr. Fuller's nickname was the "Virginia Calculator".

Malcolm X and Red Foxx

Malcolm X (born Malcolm Little) and Red Foxx (born John Elroy Sanford) worked side-by-side as dish washers in a Harlem restaurant as young men. Neither knew the other then, but they later became very famous.

Another striking coincidence about these two men is that they both were nicknamed "Red"; Malcolm (Chicago Red) and Foxx (Detroit Red), because of their red hair and fair complexion. You may also be surprised to know that Foxx was more than just a comedian and actor. He was also well known for fighting racism ... in the entertainment industry.

Rosa Parks

Rosa Parks had been forced off a Montgomery city bus 12 years earlier by the same driver that had her arrested in 1955. After the first encounter with the driver, Ms. Parks avoided that driver's bus altogether ... until 12 years later in December when she failed to notice as she entered the bus that he was the driver whom she had the encounter with years earlier. Both incidents were entirely unrehearsed. As a matter of fact, Ms. Parks says herself, "I had planned a full weekend and was not anticipating being arrested on that eventful day of December 1, 1955. It was December, Christmas..." Ms. Parks goes on further to say "I was in a hurry and was not paying attention when I boarded that bus with the same driver." Furthermore, it was common for White bus drivers to drive off and actually leave Black passengers who had already paid their fares.

Native Americans

Christopher Columbus actually admitted he was a racist, and his actions proved it. Of course, he never discovered America. Columbus' poor navigational skills caused him to become hopelessly lost at sea. His ship floated to the Americas by pure chance. As a matter of fact,

Columbus named the original inhabitants of the "New World" Indians because he erroneously thought he had reached the East Indies! The ancestors of the Native Americans literally discovered America by walking there from Asia across a land bridge before the continental drift.

When Columbus arrived in America, he sadly brought with him syphilis, and other deadly bacteria and viruses, to which the Natives had no immunity against. Thus, Columbus infected every single Indian he encountered with these horrible diseases and they (Columbus' miserable diseases) killed the Native Americans by the thousands and hundred thousands ... by way of an exponential effect. This was, indeed, bad.

Even worse, Christopher Columbus barbarically killed every single Indian in his sight when he arrived in America ... mercilessly murdering entire Native American tribes. Common practice for school books regarding African American and Native American History, trusting school children have been deliberately deceived for many years by being taught that all Indians were wild and savage, and that the White man had to kill them for self defense. The exact opposite is true. But not only did the White man nearly kill off all the Native Americans, by disease and heinous violence, they also killed the buffalo, essential to the Indians' survival, to near extinction.

America today is by far the most violent industrialized country on the planet. In fact, America's violent history can be traced directly back to Columbus' arrival and his mass killing of every Indian in his sight.

Black Sailors

Black seamen (sailors) were with Menendez when, in 1565, he built the second city in America, St. Augustine, Florida. Pensacola, Florida was the first settlement. Black seamen were also with Balboa 1513-1515, Cortez 1518-1521 and Desoto in 1540.

Crispus Attucks

Crispus Attucks made the first down payment (with his life) for "America" at Boston on March 5, 1770. Peter Salem made another payment with his life at Bunker Hill, June 17, 1775, when he turned the tide of battle by killing the British Commanding Officer Major Pitcairn. Since then, valorous African American men and women have paid with sweat, blood and tears, all the way to Operation Desert Fox, and have never produced even a single traitor to the Flag! How many African Americans today actually live as "Americans"?

Dr. Dan

Have you ever heard of a physician known as Dr. Dan (Daniel Hale Williams)? Chances are ... you have not.

Dr. Dan was not just another physician. He was a very distinguished Black physician from Chicago, Illinois in the late 1800's. Dr. Dan should be known for the first successful heart surgery he performed with very basic medical instruments.

In 1896 a nearly dead man, James Cornish, who had been stabbed in the heart during a quarrel at a local bar, was brought to Dr. Dan in just an attempt to save the dying man's life. No one believed the stabbing victim would survive the stab wound nor the surgery, except Dr. Dan. The only equipment utilized by Dr. Dan during the entire open heart surgery was a scalpel, warm salty water, needle and thread and a powerful anesthetic. Less than one hour of meticulous work, Dr. Dan sewed the last stitch in James' heart. The surgery was successful and the patient lived 50 years longer. He even outlived Dr. Dan!

The point is; many surgeons have performed many successful open heart operations, but it is a fact that Dr. Dan was a man who distinguished himself, incomparably, by performing the first.

Dr. Drew

Dr. Drew was born in 1904 in Washington, DC and grew up to become an outstanding athlete, excelling in football, basketball, soccer, swimming and track. He was also a member of the Alpha Omega Alpha Fraternity. Dr. Drew could have easily become a professional athlete but his desire to become a physician was much greater.

Dr. Drew researched a process of blood preservation at Columbia Presbyterian Hospital in New York City. While at the Presbyterian Hospital he developed a technique for the long-term preservation of blood plasma. Dr. Drew eventually earned his Doctorate Degree of Science in Medicine in 1940.

Dr. Drew's new discovery saved thousands of lives in World War II and it became the basis for the blood supply program in the American Red Cross. Dr. Drew received numerous honors and awards for his new discovery, including the NAACP's prestigious Spingarn Medal. However, Dr. Drew resigned from his position after the War Department sent out a directive, stating that the blood drawn from Black donors should not be mixed with that of White donors. This issue was responsible for a great deal of controversy. Dr. Drew responded to the matter as a "stupid blunder" and returned to Howard University, in Washington, to instruct surgery. LaSalle Doheny Leffall, Jr. was one of his students.

It is; however, quite sad to say that Dr. Drew's life was short-lived. On April 1, 1950, Dr. Drew and three of his Howard University residents departed the nation's capitol at 2:00 am to a medical symposium at the Tuskegee Institute in Tuskegee, Alabama. Dr. Drew had just given a speech the evening before and he was already exhausted from performing surgery even before he left Washington, D.C. Dr. Drew; however, decided to drive because his residents could not afford the train and he eagerly wanted them to attend the symposium. En route to Tuskegee, in Alamance County (Burlington), North Carolina, Dr. Drew's fatigue overcame him ... he fell asleep at the wheel. By the time he awoke it was too late. As Dr. Drew made a desperate attempt to maneuver the vehicle back onto the highway, the car flipped several times and ejected him. In the process, the car ran over Dr. Drew. The three physicians travelling with him were unhurt but Dr. Drew was severely lacerated and hemorrhaging profusely. One of his legs was nearly severed. *He was in immediate need of a blood transfusion.* A hospital was proximal to the accident site and Dr. Drew was rushed there. When he arrived at the hospital he was still alive.

The hospital that Dr. Drew was taken to was all White, but contrary to popular belief, he was not denied medical treatment. The hospital was small and rural, and it did not have the blood plasma procedure developed by the respective physician. Had the blood transfusion technique been available at that time, it is possible that Dr. Drew could be alive at this time. Dr. Drew bled to death soon after arriving at the Alamance County hospital. Besides the entire world, his lovely wife, three daughters and one son mourned his death. Did you know about Dr. Drew?

Other Sources

For more information on these and other facts about outstanding African Americans, read J.A. (Joel Augustus) Rogers' *100 Amazing Facts About the Negro - With Complete Proof* (ISBN: 0-9602294-7-7; check with your local library or bookstore) and visit the FAMU Black Archives in Tallahassee, Mooreland Spingarn Research Center at Howard University and the Shomburg Research Center in New York.

A Letter

Dear Dr. King

Dear Dr. King

Clinton L. Black
123 Freedom Street
Anytown, USA 12345

Dr. Martin Luther King, Jr.
3 Promised Land Lane
Heaven

Dear Dr. King:

It is with utter disgrace that I pen this cold correspondence to you ... as I shamefully describe the abject reality of America today. I am literally scared to tell you that your sweet "dream" has today transformed into the reality of a bitter nightmare! And as bad as this actual tragedy really is, it is unfortunately made even worse by the sad fact that the White man is not doing it to us anymore ... we are now doing it to ourselves! We have not overcome, yet. As a matter of fact, through our exact apathy and negligence, we as a Black people have actually gone under even deeper!

America is confused, Dr. King, and its weary people have changed quite markedly since you were ruthlessly cut down by a racist sniper's high-powered bullet in 1968. Racial inequality was, indeed, very bad when you were here relentlessly fighting it in the turbulent 50's and 60's, but I am deeply saddened to tell you that it is much, much worse now. Pure hatred among the races in America has this country so fiercely divided, you can plainly see it in our schools, jobs, community, and as you so eloquently explained, especially in the churches on Sunday mornings at 11:00.

The largest race riot in the history of "America" took place in Los Angeles in April 1992. It was caused when several LA cops were unjustly exonerated for severely beating a Negro motorist named Rodney King.

Further dramatic proof that America is more racist now than ever was clearly demonstrated as Negroes and Whites became categorically separated when former NFL superstar O.J. Simpson was found not guilty for allegedly killing two White people in California in 1994. The unfortunate reality is, Dr. King, racism has a very hopeless grip on America, still!

Poverty is also worse, and worsening. Over 11 million more Americans, mostly Negroes and Native Americans, live in poverty today than when you were taken from us in 1968. We irresponsible, selfish and broke Negroes are still laying up making all these babies, with hardly any effort, but have extremely serious problems giving our own children essential time and patience to take care of them and raise them right. The sad reality is that we immature "adults" are constantly betraying our partners and abandoning our children. There are literally thousands of shattered marriages and families every single day in this country. The majority of Negro households are headed by exhausted single mothers or unmarried couples. Domestic violence is totally out of control. Sorry Negro boys beat and cheat on their children's mothers but flatly refuse to commit and pay child support!

Idle Negro women have invented and perfected gossip, which further fuels the raging fire that is so devastatingly incinerating the once-cherished Negro marriage and family. Too many of us have completely abandoned and betrayed commitment, trust and love. According to some brother walking down Georgia Avenue in D.C., my sister is positively a bitch. Now, the sacred Black marriage and family institution is today on the warm threshold of becoming extinct!! Brilliant young Negro children growing up in despondent inner cities and unpromising country sides face a mercilessly blunt future of these brutal realities, if they have a future at all.

Crime! Sir, crime did not even exist in 1968 as it does here and now. Dr. King, even as I chirograph this very letter to you, there is a very real and clear danger that any given American will become the victim of a serious crime at any time. And I'm not talking about a petty theft or a simple assault, I'm talking about the everyday and everywhere reality of random and diabolic murder. I'm talking about strong-arm robbery, outrageously wicked rapings and pandemic child abuse. Black-on-Black crime is now so absolutely devastating, we as a Black people are more likely to be killed by a family member than even a perfect stranger! In Jacksonville, Florida, one of our brothers killed another brother... arguing over a chicken wing!!! What is our value? What is the purpose of we as a Black people?

We trust each other to no beginning. We hate one another to no end. We as a Black people gossip, lie and envy our brothers and sisters to death. This is our greatest sin.

The Civil War has long been over, but we are all still slaves! We can no longer blame the White man because our very own stupidity is today our masters. We as a genocidal Black people are all messed up today, Dr. King. We are really sick and we need help, bad.

We ignorant Negroes have murdered and paralyzed far more of each other this year alone than the Ku Klux Klan has in all of its existence!!! Twelve year-old boys with colostomies depressingly push themselves around in their wheelchairs on inner city streets and country dirt roads. Over 33% of America's Negro males are in prison or on parole or probation! And too many of those who are not locked up are jobless! I can understand why little White grannies frantically clutch their purses and sprint to the security of their luxury sedans when they find themselves approaching me in shopping center parking lots. Dr. King, I, with most profound regret, submit to you it is true that gorgeous Negro adolescents across the whole country are literally planning their own premature funerals.

Everything you ever stood for: human dignity, respect, love, peace, understanding, tolerance, integrity and simple moral uprightness are all nearly bleached bones in America now. You died in vain?

Dr. King, education in these United States has failed outright. Homelessness has worsened. The scarcity of descent paying jobs is married to unbridled inflation. AIDS, a pestilence disease you obviously never heard speak of, is today the number three caller of death. The federal budget deficit is so severe, the government actually shut down two times in as many days.

On Wednesday, December 16, 1998, the Honorable William Jefferson Clinton gave the nod to bomb Iraq (Operation Desert Fox). On Saturday, December 19, 1998, the United States House of Representatives voted to impeach the President for "high crimes and misdemeanors". China, fresh out of Third World dereliction, is now tapping "America" on the shoulder to displace it as the world's super power.

Lazy and unprofessional Negro "business" men and women routinely convince faithful customers that the White man's ice really is colder. The fact that there are now more Negro millionaires, mayors, Congress men and women, senators, state legislators, Ph.D.s, M.D.s, J.D.s, military officers and filthy rich athletes and entertainers is absolutely irrelevant when 11 million Negroes in "America" remain hopelessly locked in a vicious cycle of irreversible poverty and crime!!!

Our children are taking more beepers and weapons to school than books and pencils. They have learned from too many adults to load their sacred temples with alcohol and dope. Some Black parents simply do not care anymore and many Black youths have regrettably given up forever on education and knowledge. There are one million teenage pregnancies every year in America. Half of them are ours. I am perfectly a nigger, according to some of my students.

Only with rare exception, our Black children more than any others aggressively reject teaching and habitually molest the hallowed learning process in the public schools. White educators attempt at all costs to avoid instructing such disruptive colored children and Negro educators are, understandably, following suit. To make this unfortunate reality even more hopeless, it is too often impossible for committed teachers to bait irresponsible parents to their child's school for even a simple conference. In an especially real sense, Dr. King, what slavery, Jim Crow and lynching did to us yesterday, we as a Black people are doing tenfold to ourselves today! Sad.

If God Almighty does not personally intervene, I calculate that we as a cursed Black people, by way of our personal and deliberate choices and actions (the devil don't make us do anything), will self-destruct in three score and 10, become extinct and exist no more.

Dr. King, the last I heard, Mrs. King and your fine children are all doing well. Marty was recently elected as president of the SCLC! Still, though, you have no grandson, as of yet, to carry on your mighty name.

That "sick White brother", which you so precisely prophesied, was a petty thief and drifter, with an extensive small-time criminal record, named James Earl Ray. Ray was tried and convicted of murdering you, even though he later recanted his confession. Ray even told Dexter, face-to-face, "I did not murder your father". Ray died on Thursday, April 23, 1998.

Also in 1998, your family requested that the US Department of Justice reopen the investigation into your assassination. In spite of serious resentment from many of your former aides, your family steadfastly believed Ray. Mrs. King and your children believe that you were assassinated by a slick, high-level US Government conspiracy!

Sir, in the 50's and 60's, you made very substantial racial progress. Today, America needs one thousand of you just to accomplish half that much. I shall keep you posted.

Sincerely,

Clinton L. Black

P.S. *Please give my regards to Jesus, Malcolm and Timothy.*
Have you met an angel named Claude Neal?

BIOGRAPHY

Mr. Claude Neal

T. Thomas Fortune

Mr. Claude Neal

Southern trees bear strange fruit,
Blood on the leaves and blood at the root,
Black bodies swinging in the southern breeze,
Strange fruit hanging from the poplar trees.

— *author unknown* —

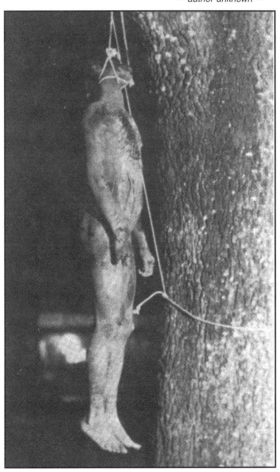

Fig. A. Picture of the corpse of Mr. Neal swinging from a poplar tree at the Jackson County Courthouse. This picture was later sold as a postcard.

From NAACP, The Lynching of Claude Neal, courtesy of the National Association for the Advancement of Colored People.

Tracks of the devil ... Saturday, October 27, 1934, 3 o'clock a.m., the sadistically mutilated body of a perfectly innocent Mr. Claude Neal hangs pitilessly from a poplar tree on the east side of the Jackson County Courthouse in Marianna.

On Saturday, October 27, 1934 at 3 o'clock a.m., it can be said without hyperbole that one of the most egregious travesties of justice to all people in the history of the United States of America occurred in Marianna, Jackson County, Florida. A fiercely enraged White mob mercilessly tortured and lynched a perfectly innocent Black man, paradoxically, on the very grounds of the Jackson County Courthouse.

Inasmuch as a single lynching is far too many, albeit routine in the South after the slaves were freed, this particular ungodly lynching of a friendly, kind and gentle Mr. Claude Neal in Marianna, Florida was one of the most recent and the weirdest in American history.

Mr. Claude Neal was born in Malone, Florida in 1911. At the time of his unearthly murder, he was 23. He was falsely accused of raping and murdering a White woman (Lola Cannidy), the daughter of one of his employers, on October 18, 1934. Mr. Neal was immediately jailed after the body of the woman was discovered. Only token gestures, the Jackson County Sheriff arranged for Mr. Neal to be shuffled among several nearby county jails to resist "mob violence". It was inevitable.

On October 26, in the wee hours of the morning, three car loads of sly White men cunningly entered the Brewton, Alabama jail and cowardly abducted innocent Mr. Neal. They drove him back to Jackson County, where they kept him bound and guarded for about 19 hours.

At around midnight, Mr. Neal began to accept unimaginably demonic torture at the anxious hands of the racist White mob. Among many other astoundingly horrific indignities, the White mob barbarically castrated Mr. Neal, like a hog! They revoltingly severed his penis, too. The atmosphere was that of a wild festival!! The ecstatic White men forced Mr. Neal to physically eat his own penis AND his testicles!!! He was then literally forced to say he liked it!!! He was savagely seared with a red-hot iron from the crown of his head to the soles of his feet. He was repeatedly hung in a tree until near death, at which time he was let down and the sadistic cycle would persist.

Even little White tots, barely able to walk, were actually taught by the adults to pierce Mr. Neal's unrecognizable corpse with sharpened sticks!!!

At 3:00 am, Mr. Neal's body was brought to the east side of the Jackson County Courthouse and lynched yet again. It got even worse.

Among the thousands of cruel and barbaric lynchings in the South, Marianna, Jackson County, always proudly maintained the commanding lead in Florida. Some were even lynched while still in their military uniforms! This lynching example, set in 1934, instilled such a paralyzing fear in the Jackson County Negroes then, it has actually passed down through the generations and endures obviously and effectively in Jackson County African Americans now.

According to Southern tradition, a "typical" lynching was not complete until:

1) a notice was sent out to all neighboring towns, so they could witness the lynching;
2) a huge spectacle with thousands watching;
3) the burning of the victim, usually a male, at the stake, after first being exposed to hours of wrathful pain, known as "surgery below the belt", and, as if that wasn't bad enough;
4) the observers took parts of the mutilated body as souvenirs and took pictures for postcards.

Mr. Claude Neal's lynching was by no means typical.

The details of the ghoulish disgrace described herein is based on *Anatomy of a Lynching - The Killing of Claude Neal -*, by James R. McGovern. For more information, read this book.

In 1997, I launched an "irreversible commitment" to officially document this most relevant history of Mr. Claude Neal in the Russ House Historical Museum in Marianna.

Fortune

T. Thomas Fortune

Friday, October 3, 1856 - Sunday, June 2, 1928

T (Timothy) Thomas Fortune, the most brilliant, committed and effective journalist and civil rights leader, was born a slave in Marianna, Florida.

Forced out of the town by death threats from the Ku Klux Klan, due to his father's (Rep. Emanuel Fortune, Sr.) ambitious progress as a Reconstruction State Legislator, Fortune never returned to Marianna. In spite of the unimaginable indignities he suffered as a child slave, Fortune miraculously persevered and literally made international achievements and contributions in education, writing, economics, politics and poetry. T. Thomas Fortune is inarguably one of the greatest Americans who ever lived.

Fortune found the first civil rights organization (National Afro American League), a forerunner of today's NAACP, in the United States in 1888. He initiated the movement to integrate the New York City Public Schools. He was instrumental in forming the 369th Black Infantry. He even coined the term "African American"! His scathing speeches were so fantastically moving, they made even the most apathetic flinch! His flaming editorials were so remarkably powerful, they penetrated the White House. President Theodore Roosevelt was once quoted as saying "Tom Fortune, keep that pen of yours off me!!!" Even further, Fortune was appointed to special assignments by presidents.

Fortune was a relentless, agitating, powerful political maverick. In order to make American justice actually materialize into a reality, Fortune said "...fight fire with fire..." He fearlessly condemned all possible forms of racial discrimination and uncompromisingly demanded full and equal opportunities for all Americans. His severe militancy made him a highly controversial man. Still, though, he used his famous newspaper, *New York Age*, to ceaselessly promote civil rights, equal opportunity, education, and harmonious race relations and vigorously oppose oppression and political and legal inequalities. His very purpose in life was to fight with all his might against such egregious injustices as those that caused Mr. Claude Neal his innocent life.

Fig. B. *Jet Magazine* story, September 4, 1995. Courtesy of Johnson Publishing Company.

After an exhausting life irreversibly committed to the cause, T. Thomas Fortune, hailed as "the beloved dean of Negro journalists" and "the ablest and most forceful writer ever", died in obscurity and is virtually forgotten today.

Currently, there is an organized effort for the US Postal Services to produce a timely Black Commemorative Stamp in appropriate recognition of Fortune. Your support is needed and requested. Please help commemorate this distinguished American by simply writing a letter of support, today, to the following address:

THE GOVERNOR OF THE STATE OF FLORIDA

LAWTON CHILES

IN RECOGNITION

WHEREAS, Mr. Timothy Thomas Fortune was born into slavery in 1856 in Marianna, Florida; and

WHEREAS, he was a world renowned journalist whose writings revealed his love of the South though they blasted its racism, and he authored three books; and

WHEREAS, he was a pioneer civil rights activist, and he founded the Afro-American League in 1890, the first human rights organization in the United States.

NOW, THEREFORE, I, Lawton Chiles, Governor of the State of Florida, do hereby recognize the outstanding contributions made to our state and nation by MR. TIMOTHY THOMAS FORTUNE.

IN WITNESS WHEREOF, I have hereunto set my hand at Tallahassee, the Capital, this 18th day of April in the year of our Lord nineteen hundred and ninety-five.

Lawton Chiles
GOVERNOR

Document 1. Honorary Resolution for Fortune. Signed by Governor Lawton Chiles, April 18, *1995*.

United States Postal Services • Stamp Services for T. Thomas Fortune
475 L'Enfant Plaza, S.W., Room 4474 E.
Washington, D.C. 20260-2435

In the Spring of 1990, I launched a major research and awareness project on T. Thomas Fortune. The factual information I learned about him was nothing less than astonishing. Fortune is clearly one of the greatest achievers and contributors in the history of the United States of America.

During the zenith of my research I submitted a proposal to the City of Marianna, requesting a commemorative statue of Fortune be appropriately funded and erected in the city. My proposal was swiftly dismissed on the grounds of a lack of funds in the city coffers.

Not one who accepts discouragement, for a solid five and a half additional years I relentlessly committed through an incredibly arduous process of frequent blows to get Fortune honored in Jackson County.

At one point, in 1991, the City of Marianna approved another

April 17, 1995

Mr. C. L. Black

In Re: Fortune Memorial Signs

Dear Mr. Black:

Please be aware that the Jackson County Sheriff's Department is deeply concerned about all memorial signs in Jackson County. The Florida Statutes contains laws, which provide for strict punishment for vandalizing or stealing of these signs.

I want to assure you that any damage to or removal of any memorial sign(s) is a serious crime, and the person or persons responsible will be prosecuted and punished to the fullest extent of the law.

Our patrol units will be checking these signs, just as often as we do all other signs and property in Jackson County.

Sincerely,

John P. McDaniel
Sheriff

JPM:cbw

Correspondence 1. Jackson County Sheriff assuring protection of the Fortune Memorial Signs.

Fig. C. Vandalized Fortune Memorial Sign, July 16, 1995. Photographed by Clinton L. Black.

proposal to have the Marianna Federal Building (Post Office) named in honor of Fortune. Inevitably; however, vehement protest from certain Marianna citizens and corrupt politicians involved in the respective legislation conspired and ambushed this progress. A citywide referendum was later held, instead. The referendum to name the

VOL. 72, NO. 150   12 Pages, 2 Sections — 35 cents

JACKSON COUNTY
FLORIDAN

Friday, July 28, 1995

Marianna, Fla.

Black thinks harsh punishment is appropriate for sign vandals

By CHRIS BRYANT
For the Floridan

Clinton Black, who spent five years working to get approval for a sign honoring a Jackson County civil rights activist, said Thursday he was not angered when vandals damaged the sign recently, but said those responsible for the destruction "deserve to die."

Two signs which read "Birthplace of T. Thomas Fortune", a Marianna-born civil rights activist, were erected earlier this month on both ends of the county along U.S. Highway 90.

The sign near on the county's eastern border was shot full of holes and black paint was sprayed on its surface said Tommy Speights, the Department of Transportation's District Public Information Officer.

Black said he was expecting the destruction and was told by telephone Tuesday evening his expectations were met.

"I was wondering why it took so long for them to vandalize it," Black said in response to the vandalism. "I'm too intelligent to be angry. And I will not be surprised if it happens again."

'I'm too intelligent to be angry. I will not be surprised if it happened again.'

Clinton Black

Timothy Thomas Fortune was born into slavery on Oct. 3, 1856, according to published accounts of his life. After he was freed from slavery, Fortune worked as a printshop apprentice at the Marianna Courrier newspaper before moving to Tallahassee and working for that city's newspaper.

He would later move to New York and became owner of The New York Age. He would also publish three books and found the National Afro-American League in 1890 — said to be the first human rights organization in the United States.

Speights said the reason why the sign was defaced — and who did it — will remain a mystery.

"We have numerous signs that are vandalized throughout the county," Speights said. "It's a shame that people have nothing else to do."

Both signs were specially-made at a cost of about $126 and the destruction magnifies the costs. "It costs the taxpayers money," Speights said.

Chris Conner, who oversees the DOT's maintenance engineering department, said a new sign should be installed in two to three weeks.

Article 1. July 28, 1995 article publicizing Fortune Memorial Sign vandalism.
Courtesy of *Jackson County Floridian*.

post office the T. Thomas Fortune Federal Building (H.R. 3100) was defeated 467 to 126 on November 26, 1991. Clearly, some registered voters supported the referendum, but most went out only to ensure its demise.

On July 11, 1995, I was successful in having the Florida Department of Transportation erect memorial signs for Fortune at the east and west borders of Jackson County on US Highway 90. The signs simply read: "Birthplace of T. Thomas Fortune" (See JET article [Fig.B.]). In spite of the Jackson County Sheriff's clear assurance of protection for the Fortune Memorial Signs and prosecution "...to the fullest extent of the law" of anyone responsible for vandalizing them (Correspondence 1), less than five days after being erected, the east county line sign was destroyed by an unknown criminal(s) (Fig.C.). After repeated requests to the Jackson County Sheriff to investigate the crime, the department flatly and firmly refused all my requests. The destroyed sign was eventually replaced.

In 1997, I also launched major projects to have Fortune formally recognized in the Russ House Historical Museum in Marianna.

PART II

POEMS

LYRICS

RAPS

QUOTES

&

A PLAY

> **POEMS, LYRICS &**
>
> **A CHRISTMAS PLAY**

Holidays & Celebrations

Rev., Dr. Martin Luther King, Jr.
January 15

Thanksgiving
Last Thursday in November

Christmas
December 25

The Rev., Dr. Martin Luther King, Jr.

I Dreamt I Saw The King

I dreamt I saw the King.
But his last seen features had changed.
He had grown gray hair, a beard,
And attained a thinner frame.

He was wearing the same suit
That he wore to his tomb.
Though his eyes were darkened now,
They were the same eyes that closed at his doom.

The King was standing on a cloud.
He didn't say a single word.
But just by seeing the "Prince of Peace",
It seemed so much that I heard.

He was just looking all over the world
And he appeared to be at rest,
Because he showed no feelings of pain,
Even though he was bleeding from his chest.

But, suddenly, the blood stopped flowing,
And then I was really surprised,
Because the King cried, "Oh God... my people!!!"
And tears fell from his eyes.

Thanksgiving

This Day of Thanks

This is the season of family days.
Thanksgiving is the first we share.
It should encourage us to be a loving people,
Because Thanksgiving is for the giving of care.

The gracious season is upon us.
It is an occasion of thankfulness as we give...
Remembering the blessings of our harvest
From God, so that we may live.

The Thanksgiving holiday is special,
In that it reminds us of our past.
It teaches us to be thankful people,
To make our blessings from God last.

I can feel the spirit of Thanksgiving.
If it is present, it can be conceived.
Just open your heart to this gracious occasion,
Then you, too, will believe.

Thanksgiving is right and at the best time of the year.
Families keep warm together
And bless the fall harvest
When Thanksgiving gets here.

We can all come together
And share like loving families should.
We can praise the God-given grace
That makes these blessed moments so good.

I say let's live like loving people
And come together to share.
Let's honor this day of thanks.
This is the special time to care.

This Is Thanksgiving

Thanksgiving is a family time...
To share thanks with our own love.
It's when we give sincere thanks
For all our blessings from above.

Thanksgiving is an intimate hour
When we give grace to God...
Thanking Him for our nourishing breads,
Our water, rains, animals and peas of their pods.

Thanksgiving is really a giving time.
It's a grateful occasion when we give praise...
Giving honor and recognition for our life.
Just being thankful for all of our God-given days.

Thanksgiving is so special.
But we only think of it when it's here.
Since this is a time for giving and sharing,
We should think of it throughout the year.

Thanksgiving is when we should stop.
Just slow our lives to take the time to see,
This is Thanksgiving...
A time for our families.

Christmas

How The Word, Christmas, Came To Be

"Daddy, I know Christmas is Christmas,
And we celebrate it each year.
But I'm curious about the Christ.
How did it get in there?"

"Mary, my little child,
What made you ask?
That's just how it's been
For so many years past."

"Yes, daddy, I know.
But there must be some way Christmas got its name.
Perhaps after Santa Claus, a great priest,
Or someone else of great fame?"

"Well Mary, my child,
You know that really is true.
But we must consider the Apostles
And the birth of our Lord, too."

"Daddy, Jesus was the Messiah
And He was called Christ sometimes.
Grandma read this to me from her Bible,
And showed it to me in mine."

"Yes, Mary, that's right.
That is really how Christmas got its name...
In honor and recognition of the birth of Jesus Christ.
That is how Christmas became."

"I see, daddy, I see!
Now I understand!!
And today, we celebrate Christmas
From all across the land."

"Yes, little Mary.
That is right my precious girl.
But Christmas is also for families
Having peace all over the world."

"Yes, daddy, and thanks.
But I have another question to ask you.
Why is Christmas sometimes written as Xmas?
What does the "X" do?"

"That is a good question, Mary.
And let's explain it to mom...
The "X" is a Greek letter,
Meaning Holy One."

"So, daddy, Christ was a Holy Man.
The "X" symbolizes His name.
It is written in different ways,
But they all mean the same."

"Mary, I'm really impressed
With your inquisitiveness about Christmas celebration.
It is good to know how Christ got into Christmas.
They have a very close relation."

"And daddy, I want to thank you for taking the time
To explain this to me,
Because I've always wondered
How The Word, Christmas, Came To Be."

Christmas Is Coming!

Seasons Greetings!
Christmas is near!
Let's display our Christmas spirit
Before Christmas gets here.

Hang up your stockings.
Decorate your home.
Display your Christmas spirit
Before Christmas is gone.

Christmas is coming.
Yes, Christmas is near!
Let's ornament our trees
Before Christmas gets here.

Let the children sing
All of the Christmas songs
Because Christmas is coming,
And it won't be long.

Lift up your Christmas spirit.
Seasons greetings to you!
Celebrate the holiday season
And be merry, too.

Send Christmas greetings
To your friends and family.
Let's make this Christmas season
The best it can be.

I love the Christmas spirit.
I can feel it in the air.
Come on everybody,
Let's celebrate the Christmas year.

Let there be joy
Across this great world.
Oh sing little children,
All boys and girls.

Christmas is coming.
Yes, Christmas is near!
We'll all celebrate the birth of Christ
On this special Christmas year!!!

Christmas Is Here!!

Christmas, Christmas,
Christmas is here!
This is that special
Time of the year.

The weather is cool.
There's a chill outside.
Our family is together,
And they are my pride.

*The lights are flashing
On our Christmas tree.
They light up the presents.
I hope some are for me.*

*The children are up early
With their pajamas still on...
Opening their gifts
And singing Christmas songs.*

*Merry Christmas, Merry Christmas!
The greetings are sincere.
I'm so glad that
Christmas is here.*

*The children are playing.
It's a special holiday.
We'll all be celebrating
Christ's birthday.*

*Oh, what a joyful occasion.
It's Christmas time!
Everyone is happy...
Everything is just fine.*

*Let's all celebrate
This 25th day.
Come drink and be merry,
In your own special way.*

*Yes, this is Christmas.
It's that time again.
There will be peace
For all women, children and men.*

*Everyone, be gay.
You have good reason to.
Merry Christmas everybody.
Seasons greetings to you!!!*

My Christmas with Bill Cosby

*Now people have Christmas wishes,
But how many are like mine?
I wanted to spend Christmas with Bill Cosby!
Was I out of my mind?*

*I was in New York
For the holiday season...
Looking for Cosby's condo,
But my friends thought I was teasing.*

*You see, Bill lives in
An exclusive neighborhood.
I knew it would be hard to see him,
But somehow, I knew that I would.*

*I made it to his condominium,
But it was still very hard.
I had to get past his Dobermans,
And the armed security guards.*

*I eased into
Cosby's condo back door.
I was walking so lightly,
My feet didn't touch the floor.*

*I rode the escalator
Up to Bill's third floor.
He was eating Jell-O Pudding
When I opened the door.*

*I said, "Hello Bill,
My name is the Poet!"
He said, "Don't tell me that,
Cos I already know it."*

*I said, "It's Christmas, Bill,
And I want to spend it with you.
Let me on your show, give me some presents,
And some of that Jell-O Pudding, too!"*

Bill said, "Let me tell you something, Mr. Poet,
Without a doubt...
I don't know who brought you in my condo,
But I'll take you out!"

I said, "Take it easy, Cos,
I'm your #1 fan!
Besides, it's the holiday season,
And Christmas is at hand."

He agreed with me
And we walked into the den.
I saw so many gifts and cards,
I couldn't comprehend.

I said, "Bill, Cos!
Look at all the presents you've got...
I don't want them all,
Just give me a lot."

He said, "Listen here, son,
Those aren't for you.
Let's go out on the lawn
And take some Kodak pictures, too."

I said, "I don't want any pictures.
Where is your limousine?
Let's go for a ride,
So I can be seen."

Bill summoned the chauffeur to bring the limo out front,
Then he said, "Now listen here kid, I'll be real blunt...
I'll take you for a cruise in my limousine.
This will be the best Christmas you've ever seen."

The driver got in the front seat.
Bill and I took the back.
We were Christmas cruising down Manhattan
In the "Cos" limo Cadillac.

It was Christmas-time in the "Big Apple"
And I was having a great time!
Then Bill said, "Are you thirsty?"   I said, "Yea!"
And he poured me a glass of fine wine.

I stood up through the T-top...
Man, I was feeling good!
I was Christmas cruising with Bill
Cos I just knew that I could...

When we arrived back at the condo,
It was getting kind of late.
Bill said, "You have to go
Cos I've got a date."

I said, "But where are my presents, Bill?
Oh!, you must've forgot."
He said, "What about the limo ride?
Wasn't that a lot?"

I said, "Okay, Dr. Cosby,
I understand."
He told me "Merry Christmas"
And then he shook my hand.

I said, "Thanks for everything, Bill.
You were so kind.
May I come back next Christmas?
Will that be fine?"

He said, "I don't know kid,
I'll just have to see.
I'm a very busy man.
I have little time that's free."

Then I left, but I was real happy
Because I spent my Christmas with Bill.
It was cool, it was off the hook!
My Christmas wish was fulfilled.

This particular encounter with Bill Cosby is fiction; however, I did have the real pleasure of meeting him at FAMU.

My Christmas Day

It's the 25th of December,
But there's no Christmas for me.
I'm alone on the streets.
This is my Christmas reality.

Homeless and hungry
On the cold streets I stand.
The freezing north winds
Have gripped my bare hands.

I cover my frail body with paper
And lie down in the park.
I'll try to sleep through the day
And awaken at dark.

But I do know that it's Christmas.
The city is flashing with decorations.
Everywhere I look,
I see signs of celebrations.

To escape the bitter winds and loneliness,
Freezing on a park bench I lay,
I shiver myself to sleep.
This is my Christmas day...

Awakened by the howling night winds,
Still in my reality,
I recapture a dream that was interrupted...
One of Christmas glee.

I had a dream that I was home
With all of my family.
We were celebrating Christmas day...
Just my family and me.

I was warm, fed and loved,
Like any human should be.
Everyone was exchanging gifts
From under our family Christmas tree.

My sister and brother were there.
Mom and dad were present, too.
Mom hugged me and said she loves me.
I said mother, "I love you".

Daddy gave me a new Bible.
It was black with gold foil.
Sister gave me a pair of mittens which she had made herself.
My sister was so friendly and loyal.

*My brother kissed me and said,
"Merry Christmas and Happy New Year".
He then gave me a beautiful necklace,
And we both broke in tears.*

*But they were tears of joy.
This was a gleeful Christmas, at home!
We then all joined together
And sang Christmas songs.*

*My little daughter gave me a green and red flower
That was so spectacular and well-grown.
She said, "I hope you like it...
I grew it on my own."*

*I then reached down to embrace my little child,
But the howling night winds awakened me first.
I thought I was with my family,
But then came the worse...*

I sat up from the park bench to recapture my dream.
But something bad happened to me.
I gathered my thoughts and realized...
I have no family.

A Christmas Play

Billy Boy, Please Come Home for Christmas

Mrs. Sue Ann Blacksmith
Rte 3 Box 125 — Peach Road
Macon, Georgia 31204

December 12, 1999

Dr. William L. Blacksmith
333 Golden Drive
Los Angeles, California 90067

Dear Billy:

Hi ya doing son. Hi is Mary and the chillins. Yall alright.

What the weather like out there. Yall warm. Billy Boy, I tell ya son, it sa cold heir. Last night it got down to therty some digrees. Ya Pa aint able to cut no moe wood like he use to. Docta told em last week he got high blood pressure and need to taike it easy now. My arms and shoulders be aching from that old orthuritos, but I get out there and fetch water and firewood. Ya Pa aint able to do it no moe ya see. He got a cold now and I do every thang I can to taike care of that for em.

What yall doing for Christmas. Can ya come home Billy Boy. Ya pa told me this morning he sho wanna see you, Mary and the chillins. You aint been home to see us since Christmas foe last. Billy Boy you no you the onlyest child wesa got. The good Lord took Charles in the cold winter we had when you was jist a baby, so you don't member em. Can you come home for Christmas Billy Boy. Me and ya Pa shall be glad to see you and I can sho use some help round the house. You no, getting ready for Christmas and everythang.

Well Billy Boy I kinda got to stop writing now cause my hand done starting aching. Ya Pa setting over there by the fire place and Isa got to get his medicine now. But Billy Boy, I sho hope yall can make it home. I'll keep praying for yall Billy Boy. Billy Boy, please come home for Christmas.

Love,

Ya ma

Dr. William L. Blacksmith
333 Golden Drive
Los Angeles, CA 90067

December 18, 1999

Mrs. Sue Ann Blacksmith
Rte 3 Box 125 — Peach Road
Macon, GA 31204

Dear Mother:

I received your letter today. Your words were most sympathetic.

Mary, the kids and myself are all fine, and we were very pleased to hear from you and father. We do; however, regret that father is ill, and you are being troubled by arthritis. I hope that the both of you will feel better soon.

Mother, I am so sorry to say we will not be able to make it home for Christmas this year. I have an extremely important executive meeting with the mayor on the eve of Christmas, and my attendance is mandatory. Furthermore, my in-laws are contemplating visiting us on Christmas day, here in Los Angeles.

Mother, again, I apologize in advance for my prospective absence on Christmas with father and you this year. I trust that you do understand my situation and I will try to make it home for Christmas next year.

In spite of my not being able to come home to you and father, I hope the both of you have a very happy and safe holiday season.

With our dearest love,
Your son, William, and family

Scene: Hartsfield Atlanta International Airport, Atlanta, Georgia
Day: Friday, December 24, 1999
Plot: Charles Blacksmith, Sr. (William's father) receives a phone call.
Time: 9:47 pm
People involved in conversation: Charles, Sr., Sue Ann, William and Bill, Jr.
Phone rings and Charles, Sr. answers, still half asleep.

Charles, Sr.:	"Hello."
William:	"Daddy, is it you?"
Charles, Sr.:	"Billy Boy! This you, Billy Boy?"
William:	"Yes father, it's Billy Boy. How are you and ma? Are you all right?"
Charles, Sr.:	"Billy Boy! Billy Boy! Billy Boy! Sue Ann, Billy Boy on the phone, girl." *(Sue Ann jumps out of her bed and hurries to the phone.)*
Charles, Sr.:	"Billy Boy, where you at, son? You out there in California?"
William:	"No father, I'm at the airport, here in Atlanta. Mary, the kids

	and myself are all on our way home. We're coming home for Christmas, father."
Charles, Sr.:	(Feeling a little confused) "But Billy Boy, me and your ma got a letter from you yesterday and you said you couldn't come home for Christmas because you had to..."
William:	(Cutting father off) "Yes, father, I know, I know, but there was a change in plans. I had the meeting with the mayor on Thursday instead of today and Mary's family came from Beverly Hills and spent the whole day with us. They took us to the LAX Airport and now we are all here in Atlanta ... on our way to Macon." (Sue Ann now on the phone)
Sue Ann:	"Billy Boy! You mean to tell me you and the children are coming home? How are you all going to get here to Macon? Atlanta's 88 miles from Macon. Isn't it?"
William:	"Yes, ma, but we're renting an automobile, so we'll be home about 11:30pm." (Bill, Jr. speaks to Sue Ann - grandmother)
Bill, Jr.:	"Hello, grandma."
Sue Ann:	"This you, Carol?" (Bill, Jr.'s older sister)
Bill, Jr.:	"No, grandma. This is Bill, Jr."
Sue Ann:	"Little Billy Boy! How are you doing, son?"
Bill, Jr.:	"I'm fine, thank you."
Sue Ann:	"Good boy, good. Grandma so glad to hear your voice. Where's Carol and James?" (Bill, Jr.'s younger brother)
Bill, Jr.:	"They're all here, grandma ... grandma?"
Sue Ann:	"Yes, son."
Bill, Jr.:	"Santa Claus is going to get me a computer for Christmas! May I teach you how to use it, grandma? May I?"
Sue Ann:	"Yes, son, you can teach grandma how to use your computer."
Bill, Jr.:	"Grandma, daddy wants to talk to you again, but I'll see you in a little while, ok grandma. Tell grandpa I brought a present for him." (William returns to the phone)
William:	"Okay, ma, we're all on our way home now. We'll be there soon."
Sue Ann:	"Billy Boy, son, I'm sure glad you all can make it home. I kept praying that you would."
William:	"Thank you mother, I'm glad that you did. And mother..."
Sue Ann:	"Yes, son."
William:	"Mother, I love you, and I'm on my way home, for Christmas."

POEMS & LYRICS CONTINUED

Love

Marriage

Personal

Rap

Social

African American

Religion

Philosophy

Love

I Love You

I love you so much...
Far more than words can say.
Darling, my love for you is crucial,
And it grows more each day.

My love for you is sincere.
All my love is true.
There is nothing I love
As much as I love you.

My love for you is strong.
It's as wide as the sea.
My love for you is tall.
It stands higher than any tree.

My love for you is authentic.
It's original from my soul.
My love for you is real.
It has meaning you can actually hold.

I'm serious about my feelings.
I treat you with respect,
Because I realize, baby...
You're the best love a man can get.

You Are So Charming

Wanda, you are so charming
You change rain into sunshine.
You are so charming
You make the hostile kind.

You are so charming
You make the blind see.
You are so charming
You put the "A" before "B".

You are so charming
You make childbirth pain-free.
You are so charming
You make the depressed happy.

You are so charming
You make the ignorant authorities.
You are so charming
You put the elderly in their forties.

You are so charming
You make workers get promotions.
You are so charming
You make the stressful pace slow motions.

You are so charming
You make the raging seas calm.
You are so charming
You turn darkness into the sun.

You are so charming
You put the weary at ease.
You are so charming
You make the discontent pleased.

You are so charming
You turn a merciless tornado into a summer's cool breeze.
You are so charming
You turn a cold, bitter winter into flowers, grass and trees.

You are so charming
You turn nightmares into sweet dreams.
You are so charming
You turn peasants into kings.

You are so charming
You show me commitment I can feel.
You are so charming, Wanda,
If anything good can happen, it will.

Just For Your Love

I'll do anything,
Just for your love.
If you ask for peace
I'll give you a dove.

I'll do anything, just for your love.
If you ask for a book
I'll give you a library.
If you ask for a recipe I'll give you the cook.

I'll do anything, just for your love.
If you ask for money
That would be my pleasure,
Because I'll give you the U.S. Department of Treasure.

If you ask for a new car
I'll give you a limousine.
If you ask for a second
I'll give you a diamond ring.

If you ask for understanding
I will comprehend.
If you ask for a cool breeze
I will give you the wind.

If you ask for a trip
I'll take you to the land down under.
If you ask for the lightening
I'll even give you the thunder.

If you ask for a kite
I'll give you a jet airplane.
If you're having a drought
I'll give you the rain.

If you're a little nervous
I will comfort your mind.
If you're in need of tears
I'll start crying.

*If you ask for a television
I'll give you the station, too.
If you don't know them
I will tell you who.*

*If you ask for some glasses
I will give you my eyes.
If you ask for a simple cloud
I will give you the skies.*

*If you only ask for one
I will give you two.
Handsome, just for your love
I'll do anything for you.*

I Want You To Notice Me

*Latangela, I've known you for years
But you just don't seem to see,
When I tell you I care,
You don't' notice me.*

*I find you so attractive...
Far more than I can say.
I want your attention so dearly
I go out of my way.*

*When I visit your home,
I always bring you a rose.
But you send me away
And slam the doors closed.*

*Girl, I really love you
And I mean what I say.
But why do you make it so hard for me
When I love you this easy way?*

*I've given you all
That I have to give.
I'll provide for your love
For as long as I shall live.*

But I often wonder...
Is my love in vain?
Even if it is,
I'll love you in the pain.

Please understand.
It's not hard to see.
All I'm trying to say is,
I want you to notice me.

I Just Want To Get To Know You

Pardon me, Miss, but I was just passing by
When I saw you standing there.
Maybe it was your beautiful face
That gave me the notion to care?

How are you feeling?
What's your name?
You're looking alright to me.

Now don't feel uneasy, lady,
But baby you interest me.
There is no way I could ignore
All of this beauty and body I see.

Can I tell you who I am?
Would that be alright with you?
And please excuse me if I'm making you nervous,
Because that's not what I'm trying to do.

I just want to get to know you,
And you to get acquainted with me.
Can we spend our evening together,
And find our destiny?

Why don't' you come home with me?
We'll chat over a glass of wine.
And then, can I hold you close
And tell you why I wish you were mine?

And then may I whisper in your ear,
Baby, you're alright with me?
Can I embrace you with a lot of care
And prove to you I'll always be there?

*Lady, can I tell you and show you
How much you really mean to me?
Baby, let me express my true feelings
And prove you're all I need.*

*Can I love you and respect you
And always prove my sincerity?
May I be with you and protect you
And love you eternally?*

*Let me lay you down tonight,
And give all of my love to you.
I'll take the time to treat you right,
And give you the trust to hold on to.*

*Baby, lady, honey!
It's alright.
Darling, sugar, sweetie!!
Tonight.*

*You know I have feelings for you
And my feelings are really for real.
Baby, do not pass me by,
Because you are the feelings that I feel.*

*Oh! lady, believe me.
There is nothing wrong with what I want to do.
So please accept my feelings baby, because,
I just want to get to know you.*

Give A Man A Chance

*Valoris, when the feeling is right
I hope that you'll know...
To give a man a chance,
To let his love show.*

*My love feelings are eager
To be expressed and shared,
And let a special lady know
That I've always cared.*

You are the lady...
The lady that I need.
I'll struggle for your love
And so will I plead.

I want to hold your tender hands
And always be there.
I want to embrace your warm body
And tell you I care.

Sincerity is sincere, Valoris,
And I'm sincere, too.
Baby, I'll prove my love to you
If I could just get through.

Valoris, when I think about you,
I think of love eternally...
Because that's what I can give to you,
And you could give to me.

I won't change on you, baby.
My love will always be true.
Fifty years from now
I'll still be with you.

But let's get this thing right.
Please understand what I'm saying
And realize my loyalty,
Because I'm not playing.

But the decision is yours, Valoris,
And I won't force you.
So just take your time
And do what you want to.

But if you really want to make
Your love life enhanced,
Then maybe you should,
Give a man a chance.

Lady, Let's Touch

I think about you, Jahazel.
But what good does it do?
I would feel so much better,
If only I were with you.

I dream about you, lady.
That's why I go to sleep.
It's really not the rest,
But it's you that I need.

I wonder about you, baby.
What are you doing today?
Does your heart become lonesome, too,
Whenever we are away?

Sometimes I try to forget it
And pretend that you are near.
But the fact of my reality
Always tells me you're not here.

I just don't know what to do
Because I truly love you.
But since I can't escape it,
I just might as well face it.

I mean this is not easy for me;
Accepting our lives apart.
So please, please darling,
Come closer to my heart.

I really need you
And I miss you so much.
I can take it no longer...
Lady, let's touch.

Baby, where are you?
I'm right here.
Jahazel, look for the sparkle
That's coming from my tears.

Can you see me?
I can't see you!
Baby, if you're not here,
What am I going to do?

Now I see you,
And I'm so happy.
I see you, Jahazel!
Do you see me?!!

You're The Only One In My World

*I've been to so many places.
I know I've traveled the world;
From New York to Venice,
But you're still my only girl.*

*I really cherish our relationship
Because you make our love right.
And when I'm away on business like this,
I think of you every night.*

*I hate being away from you
For these long periods of time.
But since we trust each other so much,
It always rests my mind.*

*I'm coming home to you, Shannon.
I'll be there in just a little while.
The girls in Miami are gorgeous,
But none can compare to your charming smile.*

*I'm so glad we've got the understanding,
No matter where I am, our relationship is true.
My job sends me away like this,
But your love brings me back to you.*

*I'm coming home soon.
I know I've been away far too long.
I just can't wait for your loving.
Your loving makes me feel strong.*

*Right now, I'm in Paris.
Paris is wonderful, but you're the best.
I'll be on that next flight out, girl.
When I'm with you, then I can rest.*

*Shannon, I'm on my way home now.
For too long I've been gone.
Just go to bed tonight,
 And when you awaken, I'll be home.*

I'll really be glad to see you, Shannon.
I've been missing you for such a long time.
You're the only one, lady.
You're mine, all mine.

In just a little while
I'll be with you.
You're the only one in my life.
You're the only one in my world.

All I Need Is You

I don't need no doctor's help.
I don't need nobody's prep.
I don't need to do no planning.
I don't need no understanding.

I don't need no automobile.
I don't need no salesman's deal.
All I need is you.
All I need is you!

I don't need no explanations.
I don't' need no occupation.
I don't need no telephone.
I don't even need a home.

I don't need no morning coffee.
I don't need no evening tea.
All I need is you.
And all you need is me.

I don't need no laws and rules.
I don't need no hammer or tools.
I don't need to know who is President.
I don't need a single cent.

I don't need no news report.
I don't need mail of any sort.
All I need is you.
All I need is you!

I don't need no pencils or erasers.
I don't need to sign no papers.
I don't need no endurance.
I don't need life insurance.

I don't need a time piece.
I don't need to pay no lease.
All I need is you.
All I need is you!

I don't need to go shopping.
I don't need to do no mopping
I don't' need nobody to bother me.
I don't need to play the lottery.

I don't need no information.
I don't need no taxation.
I don't need anything to do.
All I need is you.

A Love Like Yours

Sabrina, you're so gorgeous.
You're so fine. Be mine!
Let me take you to Miami.
Let's go out to dine.

I would love to be with
A woman as beautiful as you.
Those other girls may be pretty,
But I cherish your love and talents, too.

You're spectacular to my eyes.
You're mellow to my ears.
Won't you be mine?
There is nothing to fear.

You know you're a little, precious doll.
You're like a jewel to me.
Sabrina, I don't want your denial.
I need your love and beauty.

*You're just so charming,
And you need a good man.
So give me the privilege...
Baby, please, just give me that chance.*

*You're so special, like a pearl,
And I love you so much.
I can live with you forever,
Always within your touch.*

*Won't you be mine?
You can have me at will.
I want a love like yours...
I want beauty I can feel.*

A Certain One

*I'm looking for a certain one.
I'll find someone. I must.
I need a faithful companion in my life...
Just someone I can trust.*

*I'm living my own life,
But I want to share it with a certain one.
We could work together so much better,
If only I had a hand to join.*

*I just want to live a normal life.
But I don't want to live it alone.
I want to have a loving family
And live in a happy home.*

*Relationships are too precious to me
To just let them come and go.
I want an everlasting, sincere relationship
To relieve my solitary sorrow.*

*I can make it as I am,
But a trusting couple can make it better together than two singles apart.
We both can succeed together,
If we put together our hearts.*

I'm not asking for everything,
Just something I take very seriously.
I don't want to live my life alone.
I want a certain one to share it with me.

A Man Who's Still In Love With You

Hey there!
Oh! What a surprise to meet you here.
I haven't seen you
Since we broke up last year.

I couldn't believe that was you
When you walked through the door.
You sure seem to be doing well.
You're even more beautiful than before.

How have you been doing?
Where have you been all the months gone by?
You know, I've been missing you a little.
But lady, do you know why?

I really don't want to tell you this,
But I think I need to.
Girl, girl, girl...
Girl, I'm still in love with you.

Twelve moons have come.
Four seasons have changed.
I've seen a new year,
But I still love you the same.

Now, I haven't told anyone this.
You're the first to know.
Lady, I didn't want to tell you,
But I had to let my heartaches go.

I've changed jobs twice.
I've divorced one wife.
I've bought a car that's brand new.
But girl, I'm still in love with you.

I've been tossing and turning.
Lady, I can't sleep a night.
Life without you, baby,
Has been a life that's not right.

One birthday has passed.
I have to renew my license next week.
But girl, if I could just have you back,
I know, then I could sleep.

I've lost ten pounds.
I've painted the house blue.
I don't mean any harm,
But I'm still in love with you.

Please believe me, girl,
I've really tried to straighten myself up.
But I'm telling you,
Living without you, girl, has been all bad luck.

I haven't started drinking,
But I take a sip every now and then.
Girl, I'm out of a lot of things,
But love with you is what I'm still in.

I've tried so very hard
To get over our break up.
But the more I think about you,
The more I want to make up.

Oh girl! Life is moving on
And I'm trying to move on, too.
But, I just had to stop to say
"I'm still in love with you."

If you leave me now,
God knows I won't know what to do!
Just tell me, what do you do with
A man who's still in love with you?

Since The First Time I Saw You

Since the first time I saw you, baby,
I felt you were meant for me.
My heartbeat increased.
My tension was released.

Your eyes sparkled in my face.
Your smile brightened the night.
I could see your warm heart glowing.
Your heart was a shining light.

I see beautiful girls all the time,
But, somehow, I knew you were mine.
I just couldn't help but to see
The way your charm appealed to me.

I don't know where you were
For those many days gone by.
All I know is you were meant to be my girl
And I was meant to be your guy.

Now I wouldn't ever,
Never, tell you anything wrong.
I feel we were meant to be together.
We don't have to live all alone.

Girls always pass my way,
But you're a new lady through my life.
So I think this is the right time
To ask you to be my wife.

We can live a long life of love.
I'll always give you the best of me.
Since the first time I saw you, baby,
I knew we were meant to be.

Since You Left Me, Lady

Since you left me, Sandra,
Everyday has been the same.
It's just a constant life of emptiness,
And it's causing me so much pain.

Every minute has been the same one,
When you first went away.
I won't ever see the future
If all my tomorrows are yesterdays.

Oh! Since you left me,
Nothing has been right.
I haven't eaten a single thing,
And I'm restless at night.

Please, Sandra, come back home,
Because I don't know what to do.
If you don't feel like moving,
lady, may I come to you?

Since you left me,
Everything has been wrong.
I've been feeling real weak
And just so all alone.

Sandra, please come back to me, lady...
Baby, back into my sight.
Tell me what went wrong
So I can make it right.

Ever since you left me,
I haven't been the same.
Time is moving on,
But my sad feelings are unchanged.

I need you...
Right here in my face.
You are the only lady
Who can fill my empty space.

Oh! Ever since you left me,
I haven't seen the sun.
I'm just asking myself in the darkness,
What should I have done?

Lady, please come back, baby.
I'm dying and there is nothing I can do.
Please save my life, Sandra.
Let me come to you.

Everything Is All Right

Our love is precious.
I would never gamble with our relation.
Everything is all right.
We deserve a celebration.

I Love You For What You Are

Yes, I love you.
I love you very much.
I love the warmth of your hands
That give me that nice, soft touch.

I love you. I love you.
I love you so sincerely.
I love your bright, white teeth
That let you smile with me.

I love the kindness of your heart
That returns your true love to me.
I love your cute, shining eyes
That give you the pleasure to see.

I love your precious little ears
That give you the sense to hear me.
I love your slender, sweet tongue
That lets you speak so clearly.

I love your intelligent mind
That gives you the power to think.
I love your beautiful eyelids
That let your sparkling eyes blink.

I love so many things about you,
There are just too many to say.
So I love you for what you are,
And I'll love you more each day.

No One

No one will feel the pain
That you'll cause me if you leave.
No one will warm me
When I'm cold in the lonesome breeze.

No one will hear me
When I ask for you when you're gone.
No one will answer
When I call you on the phone.

*No one will see me
When I'm alone in the dark.
No one will visit me
When you and I are apart.*

*No one will be with me
At my most lonely hour.
No one will strengthen me
When I'm exhausted of my power.*

*No one will comfort me
On all my sleepless nights.
No one will console me
When nothing is right.*

*No one will dry my tears
When I cry my sad showers.
No one will bring me candy
When you no longer bring me flowers.*

*No one, but me.
Please spare me the pain.
Don't leave me, darling.
I'll take the blame.*

You Are My Lady

*I know you're my lady.
We go together so well.
I know you're my lady.
I simply can tell.*

*I know you're my lady.
I can feel it in my bones.
You're the lady in my dreams.
You're the lady of my songs.*

*I just have a deep down feeling
That you are my lady.
I have a hint from inside
That you're my baby.*

I know that you are my love.
I can see it in our hearts.
You're my companion in this relationship
And we can't be taken apart.

I have finally found
The lady that I need.
I know you're my lady.
To your love, I will take heed.

To Have A Devoted Man

I think so much of you, Doris,
And I really mean what I say.
You can always trust me, baby...
No matter what comes with my day.

My love for you is sincere.
It will never go astray.
Lady, the years will go by
But I'm here to stay.

I'll cherish our relationship
And make it richer each day.
We'll strengthen our dedication
To each other this way.

I'll love you for you,
And we'll be the best of friends.
We'll be a trusting, loving couple
Until the very end.

I'll be a man for you, Doris...
Protecting and loving you for all your life.
I'll respect and serve you, baby,
To make you proud to be my wife.

Now, cold days will come,
But I'll still be warm.
And some disagreements may arise,
But I will not scorn.

*Lady, I only have one color
And, baby, that one is true.
So you don't ever have to worry
About me abusing you.*

*I won't argue with you, Doris,
And most certainly never fight,
Because I'll be too busy
Making our romance right.*

*I'm being serious with you, lady.
I wouldn't tell you anything wrong.
I'm just a kind and gentle man
Who wants a relationship that's strong.*

Don't Know Much

*I don't know much about history.
Don't know much about APB (Biology).
Don't know anything about an English book.
Can't remember the last course I took.*

*But I do know one and one is two
And if this one could be with you,
Oh, what a wonderful world
This would be?*

*Don't know much about geography.
Don't know much about humanities.
Don't know much about ecology.
The only grades I make are C's & D's.*

*Don't know what "LUIS" computers are for.
Man, I wish my grades weren't so poor.
Don't know where the president's office is.
I think I flunked my last physics quiz.*

*Don't know when reinstatement will be.
Don't know a thing about chemistry.
Don't know why it takes financial aid so long.
Don't know why the cafeteria food is so wrong.*

*But I do know one and one is two
And if this one could be with you,
What a wonderful world
This would be?*

*Don't know much about convocation.
Don't know much about student relations.
Don't know why registration is so hard.
Don't know if I'll ever find a job.*

*Don't know much about Tucker Hall.
Don't know about calculus at all.
Don't know much about graduation...
That's a bit above my expectations.*

*Don't remember which year I came to "FAM".
Can't tell you when it's my next exam.
Don't know how to get into the library.
I never receive any of the mail sent to me.*

*But I do know one and one is two
And I do know that I love you.*

Marriage

The Only Time, I

Lady, our future is uncertain
Because we can't predict what it will be.
But I can assure you some things, baby,
A few things about me.

You're going to wonder sometimes, darling,
And maybe worry a little, too.
But you will never have to worry
About me mistreating you...

The only time I'll raise my hand to you
Will be to hold you in my arms.
The only time I'll make you cry
Is when our child is born.

The only time I won't take you out to dinner
Is when I cook for you at home.
The only time I'll raise my voice
Will be to sing you a love song.

The only time I'll come home late
Is when I'm trying to find you a gift.
The only time I'll turn my back on you
Will be to give you a lift.

The only time I won't buy you roses
Is when I've grown them myself.
The only time I won't do the chores
Is when there's something wrong with my health.

The only time I won't speak to you
Is when you have something to say.
The only time I won't love you, baby,
Is when I've passed away.

The Only Time, II

You know me so much better, now,
Than you did when I first met you.
But I would like to ascertain my love,
By saying what I will and won't ever do...

The only time I won't be with you when you're down
Is when I'm fast on my way there.
The only time I won't allow you to rest
Is when I keep reassuring you that I care.

The only time I won't help you
Is when you can make it on your own.
The only time I won't take you out
Is when you prefer to stay with me at home.

The only time I won't respect you
Is when I'm dead and through.
The only time I won't protect you
Is when there is nothing threatening you.

The only time I won't open doors for you
Is when they are already ajar.
The only time I won't warmly embrace you
Is when the cold distance between us is too far.

The only time I won't smell like cologne
Is when the perfume on me comes from your body.
The only time I won't buy you flowers
Is when I grow you roses, for my hobby.

The only time I won't buy you diamonds
Is when I simply can't afford their cost.
The only time I'll ever disturb you at your job
Is when my car keys are lost.

The only time I won't wash the dishes for you
Is when I take you out to dine.
The only time I won't go shopping with you
Is when my job takes all of my time.

The only time I won't take you to visit your family
Is when they come to visit our home.
The only time I won't take care of our children
Is when they're all successful and grown.

The only time I'll ever leave you
Is when I go to work each day.
The only time I'll ignore you
Is when I bow my head to pray.

The only time I'll ever frighten you
Is when you don't see me come into the house.
The only time I'll ever speak to another woman
Is to tell her "I already have a spouse... thank you."

The only time I'll ever abuse you
Is when I simply love you too much.
The only time I'll refuse to kiss you
Is when you just prefer my touch.

The only time I'll ever beat you
Is when I race you along the seashore.
The only time I'll stop loving you
Is to rest... so I can love you even more.

*The only time I'll ever have an affair
Is when its actually a business relation.
The only time I won't be home with you
Is when it concerns responsibilities to my occupation.*

*The only time I'll ever stay away from home
Is when I'm down at Memorial
... having crucial surgery on my heart.
The only time I'll divorce you...
Is when death do us part.*

Our Love Has to Change

*Dear...
Our love has to change.
I've been noticing it lately...
We've been acting strange.*

*We first had a life of prosperity.
But that was before the baby came.
What made our relationship weaken?
Who is to blame?*

*Now, we have a child,
And we've been neglecting each other for days.
A family can't last like this.
We've got to change our ways.*

*Let's spend a little more time with each other
And go out more, together!
Let's enhance our love life,
To make our family life better.*

*Let's talk about our wants.
Let's discuss the needs we lack.
I want us to trust each other.
I want our total family devotion back.*

*I don't like the way we're loving.
I don't consider this love at all.
What about me? What about the baby? What about you?
We've got to do something before our family life falls.*

Baby, I've really been thinking,
And I'm feeling the pain.
Our family life is not secure...
Our love life has to change.

Truly, honey, I love you.
And I love the baby, too.
But we've got to save the family...
We know what we have to do.

Since We've Been Married

When we started dating,
You were just so kind.
You opened my doors, tipped your hat,
And pulled my chair before we dined.

You were so eager to be my man.
You called me every day.
You expressed such sincerity for my presence,
And never wanted me away.

We treasured so many lovely times together.
You were here when I didn't need you.
You brought me flowers and perfume,
Even when I asked you not to.

You simply went out of your way
To treat me like a queen.
You took me to places I had never been before
And showed me sights I'd never seen.

But since we've been married,
I've noticed changes in you.
You've stopped opening my doors
And buying me flowers, too.

You seem to have lost interest
In the love we once valued most.
You no longer say you love me.
We don't even toast.

There are no more specially shared moments.
We've stopped going out to dine.
And when I asked you why,
You said it was a waste of your time.

I'm wondering about our relationship.
I no longer know where it stands.
I wonder if I'm still your lady,
Or even if you're my man.

I don't know what really happened...
You just don't seem to care anymore.
You've stopped saying "ladies first".
You tell me to open my own doors.

I guess you're saying you have what you want now...
You don't need to impress.
Well, baby, your love was a fake.
You flunked your cupid test.

And sugar, I'm not leaving you tomorrow,
I'm leaving right away.
I'm going to find myself a man
Who loves me every day.

Let's Save Our Marriage

Dear, I remember the day
When I said, "I do".
Our hearts were deep in love...
I was marrying you.

When we first started out
Everything seemed to be so right.
We never argued and fussed.
We didn't even scorn or fight.

We promised to love each other
Until death do us part.
Though we had two different bodies,
We only had one beating heart.

We trusted each other so much.
We were two lives in one.
There was lots of life in our love,
And we had so much fun.

But, today, things have changed.
I guess our true colors have shown.
And now, its destroying our marriage.
We're tearing apart our once happy home.

Let's save our marriage.
But, honey, we've got to work.
Before we can stop all the pain,
We have to first find where it hurts.

Let's go back to where we started...
Where our right turned to wrong.
We have to find the problem before we can fix it,
To make our marriage last long.

Let's work together.
I want to make our marriage last.
But let's take our time.
We don't want to go too fast.

I know things aren't perfect, dear,
But they really never will be.
That's why we've got to work to make it last forever,
Just you and me.

We have to realize and compromise.
Let us have understanding in our hearts.
I can see some disagreements, sweetheart,
But I just can't see us apart.

You know we've come too far
For us to just give our marriage up.
Baby, we can make it...
With a lot of love and a little bit of luck.

If things don't go
The exact way we may want them to,
Let's talk about it, honey.
There's always something we can do.

I want to work on our marriage.
We can both make it if we try.
I can hear you say we can make it,
But I can't hear you tell me good-bye.

I'm committed to our marriage.
God knows I want us to make it through.
But before we can make it last forever,
You've got to want to make it too.

What Am I Without You?

What is a child
Without his or her mom?
What is the earth
Without the sun?

What am I without you?

What is a beach without the oceans?
What is love without the emotions?
What is a friend without a friend?
What is a kite without the wind?

What am I without you?

What is a man
Without a lady?
What is a lady
Without a baby?

What am I without you?

What is a sheep without a meadow?
What is a pot without the kettle?
What is a flower without the rain?
What is success without pain?

What am I without you?
What is a masterpiece
Without a praiser?
What are the stars
Without a gazer?

What is receiving without giving?
What is life without living?
What is the morning without dew?
What am I, without you?

Personal

"Hello"

Since I don't tell you often,
I just wanted to say;
"Hello, how are you?
How are you feeling today?"

Sometimes I see you,
But I don't say hi.
Sometimes you leave
And I never say bye.

There is no offense intended.
I just didn't take the time.
So I just wanted to say;
"Hello, I hope you are fine."

It won't hurt me
To just ask how you feel.
All that really matters is
My concern is for real.

Sometimes we get too busy
Or it may slip our minds.
But we'll both feel more comfortable,
If we just took the time.

I don't mean for this
To be only for today.
There's always a nice word
That we both can say.

We'll all feel so much better
It we express concern for the people we know.
This is the reason why
I wanted to say "hello".

"Hello, how are you?
How are you feeling today?
Is everything lovely?
Is everything okay?"

I just wanted to say a nice word.
It's the least I can do.
Why should there be something wrong
When someone speaks to you?

I'm going to say;
"Hello, how are you feeling today?"
We'll all get along much better
If we have something nice to say.

Mommy's Little Love

Baby, you're my love.
You're all that I've got.
So my sweet, precious child,
I love you a lot.

Now, you are small,
But I'll raise you until you are grown.
I'm going to give you your mommy's love
In our cozy, little home.

No one can take you from me, baby,
Because you're all mine.
You're the love of my heart.
You make my life shine.

You're such a pretty little baby,
And I'm so proud of you.
You're mommy's little love.
You're my only love, too.

Just you and me, baby...
We're going to make it together.
Each other is all we'll need.
There are no two loves better.

I Want To Thank You

I want to slow down now...
Just to take time to say;
Without you,
I wouldn't be here today.

Sometimes I just go so fast...
Just too fast to see,
You are the one
Who first believed in me.

So I want to thank you
And tell you that I care.
I want to show you
That I'm so glad you were there.

So many times
I was far, far away.
But you still supported me.
That's why I'm here to say...

I thank you,
And I thank you sincerely.
You are a part of my success
And you're a part of me.

I just knew I had to tell you,
Because I wanted you to know.
You helped me to succeed
And you helped me grow.

But I won't ever forget you.
I know you're always behind me.
So I want to slow down, now...
Just to thank you so kindly.

Sometimes I get so hectic
I just don't have the time.
Things get so hurried.
And peace is hard to find.

I'm always moving around...
Just can't keep still.
I might as well accept it though,
Because that's just the life I chose to live.

But I'll always remember you.
Please stand by my side.
Together, we can make it.
And you'll be my guide.

A Friend Like You

You're a special, dear friend.
You prove to me you care.
You're always willing to help me...
When I'm in need, you're always there.

You're a true friend in my life.
I can forever depend upon you.
Our friendship is sincere
And it's a fun relation, too.

Your heart is truly warm.
Your compassion is always strong.
I cherish a friend like you.
I know our love will last long.

I accept your kind words.
I admire your loyal heart.
I hope friends like us
Will never depart.

Your generosity is genuine.
Your kindness cannot be matched.
You're a simple, good friend,
With no strings attached.

I honestly treasure your concern.
You're a friend who's trust is really true.
That's why I thank God for,
A Friend Like You.

What Matters To Me

I am not disappointed
By the fact that you can't see.
I care not you are institutionalized,
As long as your heart is free.

I do not feel isolated...
Knowing that you cannot hear.
Just so your love is understood,
It will always be clear.

It never slows me
When I know that you can't walk.
I will always listen to you,
Even though you cannot talk.

I'll loose no respect for you
If you can't get dressed on your own.
What matters to me is only that
Your love is shown.

I will never become impatient
Simply because you are weak in your mind.
I am only encouraged,
Because you let your heart shine.

I Want To Go Back Home

I want to go back home, now,
To see my dad and mom...
Back into the country,
Where it's always quiet and calm.

I want to sleep in my old room
And look at the family portraits on the shelves.
I want to let my body and soul rest,
And just be my own self.

I want to smell the fresh Spring's air
And walk the narrow dirt road to my home.
I want to leisure through the pasture fields,
And spend some time alone.

*I want to attend to the farm
And watch the animals as they graze.
I want to see how things have changed,
When I remember my childhood days.*

*I want to be going back, now.
For a long time, I've been gone.
I want to go back where I started from.
I want to go back home.*

My Struggle Is Too Great

*I was surviving before I met you.
I never said I needed you to stay.
I know that times are hard for me,
But I was making it anyway.*

*You come when you want to
And leave as you please.
I can live my life without yours.
I'm not begging you on my knees.*

*You just can't live off of me
And have everything I earn.
You take advantage of me,
But to you, it's of no concern.*

*My struggle is too great
To pull your heavy burden.
You're causing all the pain,
And I'm the one who's hurting.*

*I just really don't need you
If you're going to pull me back as I climb.
I want to keep on surviving...
Even if I have to leave you behind.*

If You Believe In Yourself

*If you really want to accomplish anything,
It is solely up to you!
Just ignore all of the obstacles
And acknowledge what you can do.*

*First, you must set your goals
And plan how they will be attained.
Then you should pursue them, relentlessly,
Regardless of any pain.*

*If you believe in yourself
There are no limits to what you can do.
So if you have endured the strain,
Your goals will come true.*

*Never allow boundaries around yourself.
It would be a costly mistake to you.
You wouldn't know your options
Nor what you're able to do.*

*It you wish to be a physician,
Start planning now!
If you want to write a book,
You already know how.*

*If you desire to be a teacher,
Go ahead, we need more of those.
If you would like to play football,
Go for the pros.*

*If you want to become an astronaut,
There is no reason why you can't be.
If you prefer to be an astronaut and the President,
You'll be on top of Washington, D.C.*

Just The Feel Of A Hand

*I need someone...
Someone, today.
I need some understanding,
Given in any way.*

*I'm not a choosy person.
I'll take whatever you give,
Because a love-starved life
Is not an easy life to live.*

I need some affection...
Just the feel of a hand.
Something to soothe the pain.
Anything to dry up the rain.

Just to know someone is there,
And I can find love somewhere,
Will help me to see
That there's somebody for me.

I need someone
Who will come out and say,
"I'll accept you, my friend.
I'll help you through your day."

I could make it much better
If only I could feel the sense,
Of just any love,
In my own presence.

A Lonely Saturday Night

Just sitting all alone
On a Saturday night...
Staring at the stars
And the moon shining bright.

My radio is singing
Some smooth, mellow sounds,
But I turn the music off...
It's pulling me down.

I wish I had a girl
To share this late night.
I'm a lonely man,
In the middle of the night.

If I had a girl
I would love her right,
Treat her like a lady
And hold her tight.

I'd whisper you're the only girl
In my life.
We'll be together, forever,
And you'd be my wife.

I stare at a single star
And make a wish;
"Just send me a girl,
I can't take this."

I close my eyes
And feel a woman's touch.
I knew in my wish
I didn't ask for much.

I opened my eyes
And, oh! What a surprise!!
It's taking me five minutes
Just to realize...

The girl in my arms
Was the girl in my wish...
So magnificent
I can't resist.

She holds my hand
And says she's here.
She's saying she loves me
And she'll always be near.

She says she felt my feelings
And heard my callings, too.
I said, girl,
"You don't know what I've been through."

I gave her a kiss
And she held me tight.
We talked and laughed
For most of the night...

The morning is early.
The stars are still bright.
But while I slept,
My lady left last night.

Inside I'm sad.
Outside I'm mad!
It just hurts me all over...
Remembering what I had.

I wish for her again,
But the stars are gone.
On a lonely Saturday night,
I lost a lady I hadn't known.

This Life, Alone

All through my life,
I live a life alone.
It's just a sad, solitary feeling...
Living in a lonely home.

I always try to fight
These lonesome feelings away,
But the struggle is too intense.
It's a part of my everyday.

Six billion people in this world...
Why must I live alone?
I just can't stand this feeling.
The isolation is too strong.

I'm trapped in my weary life.
Everything seems so wrong.
I wonder what I could do
To leave this lonesome life, alone.

My days go by so quietly.
The nights go by so long.
But every second is the same...
I stay in this life, alone.

Every day is unchanged.
I can't tell them apart.
My life of loneliness
Is hardening my once soft heart.

My Troubles Are Endless

*Sometimes, in my life,
I get lost in the day.
The troubles of this world
Just get all in my way.*

*Seems like everything is going wrong.
I can't find my way out!
I'm worried about tomorrow
Because my future is in doubt.*

*There are always problems and pressure.
I have to take the stress and the strain.
Nothing is getting better.
I'm always in pain.*

*But just how I'll make it,
I really don't know.
I'm scared and confused,
Not knowing where to go.*

*My troubles are endless.
There is no relief in sight.
I'll just close my eyes,
And continue the fight*

When Grandma is Gonnnnn

*After all those years,
I find myself alone.
Grandpa left me last winter.
I regret my husband is gone.*

*My children don't come to see me.
I guess they don't care about their mother no more.
The grandchildren never call,
Or even come take me to the store.*

*Just around this old house,
Each day I remain.
Living to survive
And bearing my own pain.*

*I can easily look back
And see the many days I've come.
I made it through them all,
From where I started from.*

*Grandma is old and all alone now.
But I'm sure to hold on.
The worst part of it all is no one will know,
When Grandma is Gonnnnn*

Rap

Kids Just Don't Understand

*Parents, I really don't know what's wrong
With these kids of today.
Instead of obeying us,
They listen to what other kids say.*

*They think they know it all.
They tell us they're in control.
Well, if they know so much,
How come they're not making the honor roll?*

*Kids just don't understand
What all their parents go through.
We never did all these things when we were kids,
So what makes today's kids want to?*

*I'm wondering about our kids.
They don't seem to know wrong from right.
For example, parents,
This is what my kids are like...*

*Just yesterday at home
I was vacuuming the floor.
I asked my teenage daughter to help me,
But she went to her room and slammed the door!*

*Just last Saturday
I was raking the yard.
I asked my son to burn the leaves,
But he said it was too hard.*

I don't know what's wrong with these kids.
Something just isn't right.
I have to watch the clothes my daughter wears
Because she likes to wear them tight.

Parents try to teach their children.
God knows we do.
We try to discipline them when they're disobedient
But they holler child abuse and file law suits, too!

When they come from school
They don't bring any books home.
They just empty the refrigerator
And turn that loud music on.

To all you kids out there,
Ya'll better listen to what your parents say.
If it weren't for them,
Your butts wouldn't be here today.

You kids won't make it in life...
Not on your own.
So why don't you clean your rooms
And get off those phones?

Kids, we really want to help you.
You need help, bad!
You go out late, come home early
And follow all those dumb little fads.

Your parents know what they're doing.
We were once kids, too.
But we never did the kind of things
That you kids of today do.

Parents, we've got to do something
And we've got to move fast,
Because the way our kids are going,
They'll never last.

I'm really worried about these kids.
Parents, what are we going to do?
Let's form a P.A.K.
Parents Assisting Kids, if you want to.

*So to all parents
Across the land,
Take it from me,
Kids Just Don't Understand.*

Play My Hit Again!

*I'm the Master Rapper,
Of the mic.
My rhymes are heavy.
They're never light.*

*So please stand back
All you part-time emcees.
I'm gonna blow up the mic before you bite,
Because I created these.*

*I'm coming hard.
I don't give no slack.
If you can't take my rhymes,
Then take two and call me back, Jack.*

*I'm here.
I'm there.
When I recite my rhymes,
I'll be everywhere.*

*I dump all my comp
Because they're a waste of my time.
The chumps are full of junk.
They can't compare my M.R. rhymes.*

*Here I am, battle me.
No need, you can't harm me.
You wanna try me?
Give up and join me.*

*I'm the Master Rapper.
My rhymes are "4" real.
You gotta pay your membership fees
If you wanna be a part of this raw deal.*

Before you sign up
You gotta line up.
But make sure you live up
Because you can never give up.

I'm serious.
My rhymes are mysterious.
You can understand them,
But you can't ban them.

I'm on a roll.
I'm on a stroll.
You can't top me.
You can't stop me.

They told you about me...
They said I was coming.
I took my time.
I wasn't running.

I rap alone.
I ride in style.
I'm number one on stage.
I'm at the top of the pile.

I'm coming hard.
I back up what I say.
My rhymes signify my personality,
So don't stand in my way.

I'm going back to the future.
The past don't concern me.
If you don't' know me,
Then, you better learn me.

I'm intense.
My rhymes produce heat.
I'm the fresh master rapper
With the funky-fresh beat!

I rock large crowds.
I sell out concert shows.
Where did I come from?
Nobody knows.

I went to school.
I achieved a degree to rap.
I'm not a blabber mouth off the streets.
I still have my graduation cap.

I've heard other rappers,
But they don't impress me.
My rhymes are supernatural...
The rap gods bless me.

Can you feel me?
Can you see me?
You can't thrill me.
you can't be me!

I'm different from those other kinds.
I don't just holler and spit.
I pump out original, high-powered rhymes...
The hits that never quit!

I'm "4" real.
My rhymes are vivid and clear.
My albums sell in Korea
And right here.

I'm it!
All my rhymes are hits.
My records never just sit.
On the turntable is where they fit.

I'm the Master Rapper
Of the year!!
I'm not afraid,
I cause fear.

I'm the man,
With the mic in my hand!
You're my fan!!
You want some more?

Play My Hit Again!!!

Social

Out On The Job

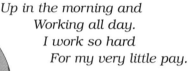

Up in the morning and
Working all day.
I work so hard
For my very little pay.

I've got bills upon bills and
Checks out that may bounce.
So I need the money.
Yes, I need every ounce.

Up in the morning,
Out on the job.
I work so hard
And they won't let me nod.

I get real sleepy...
And so tired.
But I have to keep working,
Or I'll get fired.

I see other people going to work.
Some young, some are old.
They go in the summer when it's hot
And in the winter when it's cold.

There are millions of people
Who work for a living.
They work so hard
Because no one is giving.

There are a mass of people
Working around the clock...
On the job every tick
And so hard every toc.

It takes a whole lot of people
To keep this world growing strong.
I know what it's like,
That's why I'm singing this song.

They get to work by subways, busses, cars,
Bicycles, trucks, boats, foot and train.
Most of us get little recognition.
Some get fortunes and fame.

I don't know what your job is
Or how you get there each day.
But we do have one thing in common,
We both need the pay.

Hard Working People (Like Us)

I got to work all week,
Doing the same thing all the time.
The hours go by so slowly...
Seems like it's always nine.

Trying to make an honest living
Because times get harder each day.
I hate getting up in the morning,
But I really need the pay.

It's like a clock-work system,
Just a life of routine.
If you're in the work force like me,
Then you probably know what I mean.

I look forward to the weekend
So I can rest my body with ease.
But when the weekend comes there's more work.
Typical, for times like these.

Chores around the house and
Bills to pay before they call.
Monday is almost here
And' I've had no rest at all.

They told me to "have a good one".
That was Friday afternoon.
I've had two days off,
But they ended too soon.

*Now, I'm back at the job again
And it seems like I was just here.
No vacation in sight,
But I'm glad a paycheck is near.*

*I'll keep on working
Because I must, just to survive.
But I know it's hard working people, like us,
That keep this world alive.*

My Little Smoking Song

*Here's a little song
That I created.
When we start singing it
No one can debate it.*

*Be healthy, quit smoking.
Be healthy, quit smoking!
Be healthy, be healthy
Be healthy, quit smoking!*

*Come on everybody,
I want you to quit.
Please throw away
Those nasty cigarettes.*

*It's not healthy.
It hurts your body.
Come on everyone,
Let's be smoke-free.*

*You can quit
If you really want to.
After all,
It's only killing you.*

*I once smoked,
But I gave it up.
I got tired of
That old, choking stuff.*

So come on everybody,
Put out that cancer stick.
If you keep smoking
It'll make you sick.

Smoking causes all kinds of problems,
Like bronchitis, emphysema and cancer, too!
These are only a few
Of the diseases that could kill you.

So please quit smoking.
It's not worth the consequence.
The results can be dangerous
And you'll have to pay the expense.

We all need clean air.
We need it to breathe.
So keep the air fresh,
Don't burn tobacco leaves.

Come on everybody
And sing along...
If you quit smoking
You will live long.

Every time you light up
And pollute the air,
The people next to you breathe the smoke,
And that's not fair.

So please quit smoking.
Be healthy and live a long time.
Smoking shortens your life
And suffocates your mind.

Be healthy, quit smoking.
Be healthy, quit smoking!
Be healthy, be healthy,
Be healthy, quit smoking!!

I hope you have enjoyed
My song that I created.
If you quit smoking
You will not hate it.   **Please Quit Smoking Everybody!!!**

Because Times Are Real Bad

The world sure is changing.
It's just not the same.
People's values are getting weaker
And they don't use their brains.

Weather patterns are awkward.
It was hot on X-mas day.
Even more unpredictably,
It was in the 30's in May.

Your elected seats are treacherous,
Where they sit in D.C.
If they're spending more time on trial,
Then who's manning our country!

African Americans are saying
That they are now on the rise.
If they look at the whole picture,
I think they'd be surprised.

World War III is in effect.
The battleground is our streets.
Mind the territory you tread.
The drug lords are at their peaks.

Gang violence is as common
As a family argument.
They said it's getting better,
But getting worse is what they really meant.

You must be cautious of who you meet.
They'll tell you you're friends.
But you might be enemies
When the friendship ends.

Planes are falling out of the skies
And people out of the planes.
If this doesn't make you wonder,
Then you should use your brains.

Daughter whipped mommy!
Junior robbed dad.
Grandma prays for her children
Because times are real bad.

The world is just not the same.
It's going through so much change.
We've really got problems, people,
So let's use our brains.

The Other Side Of The Computer

The world is in the computer age now.
Technology is in everything we do.
We can speed across the sky in a supersonic jet,
And press buttons for pleasure, too.

We can communicate across the globe
In just a fraction of time.
We can fly to Tokyo at six
And be there by nine.

We're living in a fast-paced society
That isn't slowing down.
There's a lot going on
As the world turns around.

On September the 29th (1988)
The American Shuttle "Discovery" returned to space.
It had a mission to accomplish...
One that would benefit the human race.

America has a new president.
Industry is advancing every day.
The world is changing so rapidly,
We sometimes loose our way.

But in the midst of this computer society,
There's a sad side untold.
The world is always warm to some.
But for many, it's bitter cold.

Too many people are unemployed.
Crime is at an alarming high.
Families can't afford insurance...
Some members die.

Housing is a major problem.
But some Russians live in space domes.
What do we do with our own people on our own planet...
Those who have no homes?

Crack is at large!
It devastates at will.
2 bad addicts wait 2 late
2 learn that crack kills!

We're destroying our atmosphere
And it cannot be replaced.
Nature is becoming more violent.
Will it destroy the human race?

The White House is in Washington, D.C.
But the homeless are there, too.
The President lives a life of luxury.
What is this world coming to?

We have problems with our children...
They don't want to go to school.
They'd rather ride the streets
And break all the rules.

AIDS, armed robbery, suicide...
It happens everyday.
Destitution, prostitution, Blacks killing Blacks...
Where will you go in a direction this way?

Starvation, poor relations, deprivation,
No education... all over the nation.
No one seems to care,
But it's everyone's obligation.

The world is advancing rapidly...
So rapidly it cannot wait.
And those who can't keep up,
Are just too late.

*I'm really not concerned about the future.
I'm worried about today!
We're living in a computer world,
But humanity is getting weaker on the way.*

Our Children

*Little children in the big cities...
So many are on their own.
Just walking the streets,
And they're all alone.*

*Their environment is cold.
It doesn't teach them right.
They live to survive.
They have to steal and fight.*

*They're on the streets
Every day and into the night...
Fighting and causing crime,
And they think it is right.*

*Little children on the streets.
Let's all help them, please!
It's not right for them to fight
Just to meet their daily needs.*

*Let's teach our children
And help them to grow.
But we have to do it today
Because they are our tomorrow.*

*Some are hungry for food.
Others are in need of a home.
Please tell me America,
Where has our compassion gone?*

*Please help our children...
For kids' sake.
Just a little bit of love
Is all that it takes.*

These kids are desperate.
They need help bad!
They've got crime, negligence and drugs.
But trust and guidance is something they've never had.

Our children are our future,
So we've got to lead them today.
We have to teach them the truth
And show them the way.

It's not just in the big cities,
It's for kids all around the world.
We have to teach them that God loves us...
Especially little boys and girls.

We all can make a difference.
Start with the children first.
If we continue to neglect our children
They'll only get worse.

Let's teach all of God's children
And give them an understanding hand...
From New York to Los Angeles
And all across the land.

Let's reach out to our children
And show them the way.
They are our tomorrow,
But we have to teach them ***today!***

Children Learn What They Live

You've heard the old saying,
"Children learn what they live."
Well, if this is the case,
Then we're wrong in what we give.

Why are our children
All going astray?
It must be their environment...
It's not teaching them the way.

A child's mind is crucial.
It's very easy to mold.
Children will go astray
If their environment is cold.

If you take a little baby
And allow uncommitted adults to raise him,
As the child grows older
He will act just like them.

*This is why children must be **positively** trained...*
Beginning even before their cribs.
Children are what they are because
Children Learn What They Live.

When You're Dead in Your Grave!!!

"Dave, I was really going to warn you about drugs,
But I guess I just never took the time.
Maybe I took for granted that
You knew using them is a crime?"

"Besides, I'm always too busy
And sometimes I just forget.
I wanted to tell you that you can get addicted to drugs,
And it will be impossible to quit!"

"But, I figured you were too young, now, son...
I had planned to talk to you about this next year.
I was going to tell you that, sometimes,
You have got to resist the pressures of your peers!"

"Your mother and I thought that
They teach you about drugs at school.
You know we love you, Dave,
But I presumed you knew that drugs were against the rules."

"You never asked us about drugs,
So we assumed you knew they were wrong!
I wanted to tell you, son, that drugs can kill,
And they destroy families' homes."

*"Dave, your mother and I don't use drugs,
So we just knew that you wouldn't use them.
I wanted to warn you that if you ever did,
Son, your future would be dim."*

*"I was really going to teach you about drugs.
You believe me, don't you Dave?
I just never thought it would be...
When you're dead in your grave!!!"*

If you don't teach your children about the dangers of drugs, it could be a grave mistake. For more information on drug abuse awareness and prevention, please contact your local agencies.

African American

... For Black People to Do?

*Black people are an interesting race.
America is where a minority live.
Oppressed by years of slavery and discrimination.
Gave to others more than they had to give.*

*Times have changed, though.
Black people have changed as well.
Once a powerful race of trusting people.
Today, their selfishness causes them to fail.*

*Some live in large cities.
Others, in places untold.
But their grounds are common, in that
They have nothing to hold.*

*Today, drugs and technology are the subsequent causes
(Of the worsening situation)
The responses are addiction and insufficient education.
The other man used to hold both legs.
Today, the above serves this operation.*

Black people would love to succeed in society
But the obstacles stand far too tall.
They're restrained by their own environments.
This self-destruction makes them fall.

With few positions in power,
They're becoming less competent in a world of progression.
This results in their stressful living.
"Hard times" are their only confessions.

Weak in "hard times"...
It's like survival for the fittest.
The weak are preying on the weak.
The powerful become the richest.

The weak prey on the weak.
Black on Black competition at an alarming increase.
The powerful prey on the weak.
The weak work for the powerful for survival at least.

Impeded by the other man,
Don't trust their own...
Destruction and self-destruction
Are the results that are shown.

Times so "hard",
They turn on their very own race.
Feeling powerful at first,
But even weaker when the consequences they face.

Surely, there are some Black people
Who have fortunes and fame,
But most do nothing for their less fortunate brothers,
Just to keep playing the other man's games.

When the powerful impedes the weak
And the weak destroys the weak, too,
Just what do you expect...
For Black People To Do?

Religion

To Fall In Love, With Living

To fall in love with living
  Would be a deadly mistake.
    How disappointing would it be for you
    If in the morning you do not awake?

All people hope for the "best" in their lives...
  In their personal respects.
    But if you were to fall in love with your life,
    A fatal heartbreak you are sure to get.

You know that life is real
  And death is an inevitable reality?
    But did you know that you are foreordained
    To a life-ending destiny?

It would be very dearly unwise
To go through life thinking you are immune to death.
For when the abrupt occasion arises,
You'll want just one more breath.

Life can be a constant struggle with misery...
No one would consider it good.
Or life can be a continuous pleasure...
Everyone wishes that it would.

If you place your values and life in this world,
You really have nothing at all...
Because there is not a single thing that can exempt you
When the obvious voice of death calls.

Never fall in love
With anything that will not last.
If you fall in love with living,
You both will come to pass.

Death is a ruthless character.
It cares not if you're a baby or 100 years old.
So fall in love with God.
He has the only everlasting hand you can hold.

Life can be a wonderful world.
But at its end, there will be no more giving.
So fall in love with the Lord.
Don't fall in love with living.

My Love Was Gone

I was away from home
When I received the sad news;
My love had passed away...
Just too bereaving to believe, so I refused.

I thought there was a mistake,
Just too distressing to conceive.
But Jesus Christ told me it was true.
It was then that I believed.

As I traveled back to my home,
Our times together leisured through my mind.
We shared a life full of love...
Interrupted by the forces of time.

I didn't question God,
Why did He take my precious love away.
I just took it as His will,
As He would take me one day.

When I finally arrived home
I was anxious to see my love.
But I wondered where to look...
In the coffin below or the heavens above.

I viewed the body at our church.
My love, lying there so still!
My mind asked "Why did God take you?"
God showed me, it was His will.

My love's funeral services were long.
There was just so much to be said.
I was quiet, but I hurt inside...
Accepting the painful fact, my love was dead.

There was a short walk to the cemetery.
My love's grave was on the church grounds.
I slowly trailed the pallbearers' steps.
My faint moans were the only sounds.

The priest said "Ashes to Ashes".
I said "Dust to Dust".
I really hated to leave my love,
But somehow, I knew I must.

The deacons lowered my love's casket into the earth
Until my love was no longer in my sight.
It seemed my grief was lowered also,
Because Jesus held me tight.

My trip back was easier.
I was leaving our home.
I had come to accept,
My love was gone.

How Did God Do It?

I stand alone in the dark
And gaze deep into the sky.
I see the moon and the stars,
And then I wonder why...

I wonder how they were created.
Did God do all of this by Himself?
The job must have been laborious.

Maybe God had some help?
The deeper I stare into the heavens,
The more curious I become.
How did God make all these bodies;
The moon, the stars, and the sun?

The universe is just so massive.
It stretches much farther than my eyes can see.
Every sight is so spectacular.
God's artwork really impresses me.

But I still wonder and I wonder...
How did God create the heavens and the lands?
I wondered again and remembered...
God has all powers in His hands.

I'm Singing A Nervous Song, Jesus

Sometimes, my dear Jesus,
This life of mine gets so weary.
I become confused Lord,
And I need someone to hear me.

Seems like the harder I try, Jesus,
The more misery I see.
I don't bother anyone, Christ,
But some people trouble me.

I try to live a righteous life
And treat everybody right.
But everyone is not the same,
And I loose sleep at night.

Trying times come, Lord,
And they try to change my mind.
Bad times are here, Jesus,
And they impede me as I climb.

Christ, it really gets rough with me.
But I'm trying to make it anyway.
I pray to you nightly, Lord.
Now, I'm praying in the day.

I'm hearing of killings, Saviour,
Everyday I live to see.
I'm singing a nervous song, Jesus,
For my own security.

People talk about me, Lord,
And I haven't done anyone wrong.
They go out of their way to hurt me...
Just won't leave me alone.

I get lonesome sometimes, Jesus,
And I have a family.
I'm in debt, Lord,
And I have no money.

I'm unsure about tomorrow
Because I'm down with today.
I always work for the best.
Give me strength please, Jesus, I pray.

Jesus, it is right to tell You
That I am lonesome and weary.
No one else will listen to me, Lord,
But I thank God You hear me.

Until I Can Pray No More

Oh my dear Lord,
It is with great humbleness that I come to You.
Jesus, I wish to give You full honor
For all the righteous things that You do.

My Lord, I just want to pause for a while,
To recognize You at this time.
I want to thank You for being so understanding,
So compassionate and, oh Lord, so kind.

I just want to respect You, my Lord.
For without You, I would not be.
I do realize, my Jesus, You have all power
And Your Holy blessings are for free.

Dear Jesus, I wish to pray for myself
And the afflicted among me.
Lord, I want to pray for the sinners,
Your non-worshippers, wherever they may be.

Almighty, let me pray for the ill
And those who do not pray for themselves.
Christ, may I pray for the liberated ones?
Please let me pray for those caged in jails.

Jesus, I wish to pray for the elderly
And I pray for the unborn, too.
Lord, let me pray for my fellow Christians
And those who do not know You.

I would like to pray for the clergymen,
The teenagers and adults.
Dear Jesus, I pray for the little children
And those following the antiChrist cults.

Christ, please let me pray for the drug addicts,
The homeless, the wealthy and the poor.
Dear Lord, please let me pray and pray and pray,
Until I can pray no more.

Dear Jesus, I speak to You with a sincere tongue.
I would never submit to You unclean.
These words that I present to You Lord
Are prayers that I really mean.

Yes Lord, I confess, I know that I need Thee.
And please help me to live a life free of sin.
Jesus, I know someone else needs You, too.
But I pray they try you. Amen.

II *? or Not* II *?*

God, it is said
You have all powers in Your hands.
Then Superior of all supremes,
Please help me to understand...

Exactly, how do You wish
For we humans to live?
Why do some people take
And others give?

Precisely, what do You expect
For we people to do
When some of us worship Thee,
And others not know You?

Definitely, where are You
In six billion souls strong?
Why do some of Your creations do right
And others do wrong?

Where are You
At one's most despaired hour?
How do You control
Your unlimited powers?

Some of Your children live to suffer
On this God-given globe.
Others wear the finest
Of the most luxurious robes.

Do You feel the pure grief
And hear the sincere prayers prayed?
How can You stand to see
Your own people plagued?

Are not You moved
To know little children starve?
Do You give inspiration
When life gets hard?

Why do the good seem to fail
And the bad, to thrive?
Why don't You intervene
When the weary take their lives?

God! Where are Thou?!!!
Man has reached his helpless day.
To keep the faith is a challenge.
But somehow, I may.

Philosophy

Life...

Life is all of the natural processes
That enables one to live.
In it are circumstances
That determine the way we live.

*Even before you are born
You grow and learn to adapt to the world.
You're privileged sense of hearing is your first,
And your last when you leave the world.*

*Throughout life, circumstances prevail
And you adjust to them accordingly.
Those that do prevail are non-selective
Because you will inevitably adjust to them accordingly.*

*It really doesn't matter
What life brings to you because
While you are living it,
It will appear that it is due to you.*

*What is in life?
Infinitely many ways in life, there is.
But it only goes one way,
And that's the way it is.*

Everybody Has A Story To Tell

*Wherever you go
And all the people you talk to,
They always have something to say.
Telling their own stories is what they always do.*

*Everywhere I go
And all the people I talk to,
They're always saying what they think they know.
They're always telling you what to do.*

*People of young and old
All have something to say;
Telling how they perceive it
In their own special way.*

*Some talk about life.
Some talk about dying.
Some tell the truth.
Some are only lying.*

Others feel whatever they say,
It's always right.
Sometimes, if you dispute them,
They'll be willing to fight.

It's a world of information.
Everyone is telling it how they see it.
Some people listen to it.
Some people believe it.

People experience all kinds of things in life
And they talk about it when they see you.
No one is going to keep silent.
They're going to tell you even if it's not true.

People simply always feel
That they have to talk.
But when the information is wrong,
It's never their fault.

Wherever you go,
Or wherever you may be,
You're going to hear people prattling,
And then you will see.

It's a world of information,
Of which very little is true.
People have infinite perceptions,
And they tell them to you.

The Whereabouts Of The Once-Lived

All those souls that once lived,
Where are they today?
Are they still around us,
Or are they forever gone away?

The past souls were once living.
They were all here, too.
I wonder if they can hear us
Or see the things we do.

Can they feel our pressures?
Are they wary of our cares?
Do they understand our problems?
Can they hear our prayers?

What are the past souls doing?
Are they asleep and never to awaken?
Are they sensitive to the earth's storms?
Do they move when the earth is shaken?

Where are the once-lived?
Are they gone away, never to return?
The whereabouts of the once-lived
Is of my concern.

We're All The Same

People are just people...
Nothing more, nothing less.
Even though there are over six billion of us,
No one is the best.

Some people seem to have it all
While others seem to have none.
Some people labor for life
While others live for fun.

There are many classes of people.
They range from the very bottom to the top.
But we're all God's children
And it doesn't matter what you've got.

Everybody sometimes wonders and worries.
That's just a simple fact of reality.
Those you see on the streets have serious problems,
But so do those on t.v.

When it really comes right down to it,
We're all the same.
Everyone wants the answers
But no one wants the pain.

Where Do We Go from Here?

It's almost the year 2000!
But I don't know when this world was created.
I guess since no one was around then
The exact time cannot be dated.

But I do know for sure,
People have been on this earth for many, many years.
And today, it's a globe full of multiple races.
But what the future holds is my concern here.

Since man first breathed the earth's air,
To this exact point in time,
Many things have occurred in every respect.
I wonder what else is on his mind.

The world is enormously massive
And there are billions of people on this earth.
There are five different races
And every split-second there is a birth.

In our society, in this world,
There are cultures and worlds we never see.
But even so, there's one thing I know,
Other people question the world's destiny, like me.

Forty-two U.S. Presidents.
Too many days gone to be said.
The earth has faced countless sunrises.
The living is the offspring of the dead.

There have been two World Wars.
America is now fighting World War III...
Fighting crime to an endless point.
There is no destiny.

People starved 3,000 years ago.
People are famished today.
Scientists and engineers have for long probed the mysteries of the world.
They're still searching for new ways.

Tornadoes and hurricanes.
Fires, earthquakes and rain.
Freezing winters and summer droughts...
A million years ago these catastrophes came.

Plagues and diseases of many names.
Accidents and illnesses claim people's lives.
It's a world going in circles.
Everyone wants the prize.

Black people have always fought for what is theirs.
They'll fight until the end.
Everything was meant to be.
Life is pre-ordained, my friend?

Technology is searching for the answers.
It's advancing every day.
It seems the closer they get,
The questions become more complex on the way.

People go to work every day...
Working on the job to keep this world moving.
Most are working just to survive.
Even some of the employed are loosing.

Although everything is changing,
Everything remains the same.
It may appear as if we're progressing.
The days we're in have already came.

Every morning I wake up,
I wonder if the end is near.
Just to search for tomorrow, we must know...
Where Do We Go From Here?

(untitled)

Over six billion people on this globe,
All living different lives.
Yet, the world operates in precise synchrony...
Probably left unnoticed, if not realized...

*People are the basics of this world
And they control it to a certain extent.
But in ultimate reality,
The world controlling us is what was really meant.*

*What determines one's fate is not himself,
But his environment and his genes.
They motivate the way we live, where we live,
How we think, and everything.*

*Since our surroundings and our past
Mold the character of our minds,
And such varies infinitely,
This is why such a mass of people live lives of every kind.*

*If not for our fates of predisposition,
With such an enormous world of people,
There would be an enormous world of disorder
Because everyone would be mispositioned.*

*With an astronomical world of people,
There really would be non-survivable chaos if not for our predestinations.
No one would do what needs to be done
And everyone would fail to meet their obligations.*

*It's a massive, complex world,
Being conducted by this world.
Other people ultimately influence your actions.
You ultimately influence other people's actions.*

*Everything happens for a reason!
One plus one equals two.
You can trace milk back to a cow.
You would probably find a monkey at the zoo.*

*No one can say, ultimately,
That he did it on his own..
We're all influenced by people who are here,
And some, who are gone.*

*No individual is an individual.
He is a mixture of billions of kinds.
No one controls their own life.
Your genes and environment is your mind.*

Time Is Passing By

*No matter what you do
Or how hard you try,
Life is up to you because
Time is passing by.*

*Each second comes and goes.
All the seasons change.
No matter what you do,
Time will pass the same.*

*Yesterday has come and gone.
Today will soon become tomorrow.
You've got to do it now
Because there is no time to borrow.*

*Time is passing by.
It never stands still.
Even while you're asleep,
Time stays awake until...*

*You've got to use your life
Because everyone must expire.
It's your own option
To fulfill your desires.*

*Everybody is on the clock,
But no one knows when it will chime.
This is just one of
The disliked characters of time.*

*Time is truly passing by
And there is no wondering why.
So if there is something you have to say,
You're going to have to do it today.*

And Death...

*Did you think it wasn't coming?
Did you forget about it all?
Remember, no one can ignore
The obvious voice of the death call.*

Death is the absence of all characteristic life functions.
It is a temporary state of being after your first life.
You already know that life after death does exist.
That is why, at my Love's funeral, I did not cry.

People perceive death in infinitely many ways.
I perceive it in only one.
It is just a phase after life,
Of which you will transcend from.

Death should not be taken as the worst possible circumstance.
It is a period of utmost peace.
So be consoled, griever, by knowing that you can,
Again, see your mother, brother, friend or niece.

Life is worth living
And death is worth dying.
You merely have to understand them both,
And you will cease all the crying.

QUOTES BY CLINTON

Quotes by Clinton

"Racism will always be a disgraceful disease that plagues this world. It is best treated with broad spectrum doses of education."

"New technology and advancing industry is fine, but the precious, irreplaceable environment is finer."

"There is nothing in this world going to happen that isn't supposed to. And that which is supposed to happen, will happen... for better or for worse."

"There is no such thing as magic or a ghost. There is; however, a physical reason for everything that happens and exists."

"If one sets out to achieve any certain goal in life and does not accomplish it, then he/she never was supposed to. But if one accomplishes his respective goal, it was always meant to be."

"Education and wisdom can be powerfully constructive. But without common sense, it is powerfully destructive."

"Living in this world may be a heaven to some people. But not knowing why you are living would be hell."

"It would be eternally good if every soul would be saved because, after you die, there is nothing else this world can offer you, and there is surely nothing further you can take from it."

"The greatest step towards being happy is being alive!"

"Everyone is capable of doing good. It is one's unique perception of what is 'good' that may cause him to do bad."

"The right measure of the accomplishments and quality of human life is not how you spent your money, but how you spent your time."

"... and this is the way it is: knowledge will always be the most profitable asset to this world, but ignorance is the most costly liability."

Order Form

Book Order and Receipt Form

Name: _____

Address: _____

Phone: _(____)_____

    Price per book: ____**$20**____

    Quantity: _____

    Sales Tax: **PAID BY CLINTON**

    Postage & Handling: **PAID BY CLINTON**

TOTAL: (__$20__ x ____ quantity =) $_____

Make check or money order payable to and mail to:
Clinton Black P.O. Box 9096 Fort Lauderdale, FL 33310

Thank You!

Please allow 1 week for delivery.